The Bumper Bundle Companion Workbook

Quizzes and exercises to strengthen your modelling muscles

Fran Burgess

KILMONIVAIG PUBLISHING
www.nlpand.co.uk

First published by:

Kilmonivaig Publishing, 22 Painterwood, Billington, Clitheroe, Lancashire, BB7 9JD, UK

www.nlpand.co.uk : admin@nlpand.co.uk

British Library of Cataloguing-in-Publication Data

A catalogue entry for this book is available from the British Library.

Print   ISBN 978-0-9928361-2-2

Online version available from The NLP Kitchen: www.nlpand.co.uk

Printed and bound by Lightning Source Chapter House, Pitfield Kiln Farm, Milton Keynes, MK11 3LW

Contents

Introduction

In *The Bumper Bundle Book of Modelling*, you are introduced to the principles, processes and practices surrounding the many facets of NLP Modelling. You are immersed in information and observation, supported by innovative models and frameworks, all with the intention of deepening your understanding of the nature and application of NLP's vital process of Modelling. Having absorbed the knowledge held within this book, you may have found that your own attitude and self belief has strengthened, and you have become more confident with the reasoning and decision-making that you bring to your modelling practices.

However, the knowledge and insight on offer is 'just' theory. As with all learning, you will only know if you have gained from this knowledge if your application has improved. Knowledge itself does not improve skills automatically. Skill development comes through applying new knowledge, testing it, evaluating feedback and integrating the resultant learning. It requires discovering what has been assimilated into the muscle and what is still merely rumour – to paraphrase Judith Delozier.

This *Companion Workbook* seeks to work alongside the Bumper Bundle textbook. Here I am offering you a range of qizzes to test your understanding and recall, and practical exercises to test your ability to apply your knowledge.

Most of these exercises have been created over the years and tested on our fabulous learners at The Northern School of NLP. I thank them for their insightful feedback. Others emerged as part of a series of ebooks found on our website, *The NLP Kitchen* www.nlpand.co.uk, and some found their source in the recent material within *The Bumper Bundle Book of Modelling*.

For many of the exercises I provide worked exemples, to get your thinking started. Whilst mapping across the chapters of the Bumper Bundle, I have used the Bandler model, to establish the chapters, namely:

- **Attitude:** with quizzes and some exercises on developing Identity and testing underpinning knowledge.

- **Methodology:** the topics here cover the modelling process and skills of handling relationships, working with data, and very importantly working with language – the key skill in our repertoire.

- **Technology:** the engine room of our practice and the one most apparent to acquirers. You come face to face with the nuts and bolts of our techniques, their components and relationships.

The Bumper Bundle Companion Exercises

At the back of the workbook, I offer suggested answers, totally accepting that other answers may suit just as well. If your answers differ significantly from mine, it is worth the time to explore how I may have arrived at that answer. Refer back to the Bumper Bundle textbook. If you are left totally bemused, get in touch!

After some deliberation, I have opted to produce this workbook in this format as opposed to spiral bound. This has pros and cons. The big pro is that you can see the spine on your shelf, and it is more robust. It can be opened up flat if you don't treat it too gently. The con is that it doesn't lie completely flat and some people may be inhibited about writing in a 'proper' book. Tom Peters, the '80s business guru, would refuse to sign a book without pages turned down, notations in the margins and passages underlined. 'How else would I know that you have engaged with it?' If however you can't get over your fear of book vandalism, we are providing an electronic version on *The NLP Kitchen* website, www.nlpand.co.uk, which you can print off at your leisure.

I hope you are up for the challenge. And I hope you gain a lot of learning from the materials that are here. I have thoroughly enjoyed creating them. If you gain greater clarity about the various aspects of the modelling process, and increase your confidence in the process, then the challenge I set myself fifteen years ago has succeeded. If you also enjoy the results, then I am more than delighted!

Certainly this *Companion Workbook* is a great resource for those of you who are NLP trainers and offering modelling as part of your training provision. Feel free to incorporate any of the excercises in your trainings, assuming that you always include your sources.

I congratulate you on your commitment to your NLP learning. Here's to a lively stimulating journey. And if you have any comments you want to make or feedback you think would be useful, please feel free to contact me – fran@nlpand.co.uk.

Happy playing!

Fran Burgess

April 2014

Attitude

The Personality of a Modeller

There is a clear modelling mind-set. The nature and the make-up of the modeller will determine their effectiveness. Some of us already favour some of these attributes and therefore naturally respond to the practice of modelling: while for others, the requirements seem more distant. Happily, however, all of us inherently have these attributes, but perhaps some of them need reawakening from the heydays of our childhood.

Modellers in the Field

List as many occupations as you can which hold a modelling mindset as an essential part of their function.

Attributes of a Modeller

Come up with at least three attributes common to modellers under each of the headings, and then provide a personal example of when you have demonstrated this attribute. It doesn't have to been highly significant, but enough of an example to remind yourself that you do have these resources.

Attribute	Personal Example
Mission driven	
Adventurous	
Disciplined	
Non conforming	

Funny	
Inquisitive	
Risk taking	
Practical	
Learning	
Systems minded	
Structure focussed	
Pattern detecting	
Innovative	

Your Call to Action

You may already know what you want to give your modelling attention to, and are already for the 'off!' Or you may be aware of a gap that needs filling: and when filled it could improve the lives of yourself and others. Or you may be realising that you are searching to focus on something which would be personally fulfilling and serve your sense of Purpose. This last motivation can produce some phenomenal results.

Bill O'Hanlon's model for Purpose

Looking back through your life events:

- **Pissed:** what has angered you to the point that you want to seek retribution to redress the injustice?

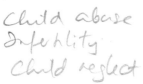

Child abuse
Infertility
Child neglect

- **Dissed:** how have you been discounted in the past and now it the time to make yourself noticed?

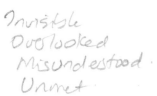

Invisible
Overlooked
Misunderstood
Unmet

- **Blessed:** how have you been honoured and sponsored in the past and you want to pass this acknowledgment to others?

Rosie
Michael
Mev Marsh

- **Blissed:** what are you constantly grateful for and appreciative of, that you want to share with others?

My home
My ideas
Amelia - hope

Underpinning Philosophy

Spending time understanding *why* we do *what* we do the *way* that we do it, is essential to inform and direct our decision making and drive the focus of our actions. Neurolinguistic Programming has its home in Constructivism, with the basic tenet that 'we create the reality of our lives'.

Quiz

1   Ontology is:

   a The Study of Knowledge

   b The Study of Being

   c A Theory of Learning.

2   Epistemology is:

   a The Study of Knowledge

   b The Study of Being

   c A Theory of Learning.

3   Constructivism is:

   a The Study of Knowledge

   b The Study of Being

   c A Theory of Learning.

4   Knowledge results from:

   a Truth, Reality, Evidence, Belief

   b Reality, Logic, Scepticism, Belief

   c Evidence, Context, Perception, Belief.

5   Forms of Constructivism are:

   a Radical, Social, Post Modern

   b Modern, Post Modern, Cognitive

   c Personal, Social, Cognitive.

6   Cognitive Constructivism was introduced by:

   a George Kelly

   b Jean Piaget

   c Ernst Von Glaserveld.

7   Personal Constructivism was introduced by:

   a George Kelly

   b Ernst Von Glaserveld

   c Lev Vygotsky.

8   Which is the odd one out? Constructivists believe:

   a We create our own personal realities

   b Relies on pre-set theories and predetermined approaches

   c All behaviour is outcome generated.

9   Which is the odd one out? Constructivists believe:

   a Our internal system of structures generates our sense of self

   b All experience is experienced through the senses

   c Structures are fixed and laid down.

10 Which is the odd one out? Bateson is the source of:

   a There is no such thing as a resistant person

   b All our life experiences are encoded in our neurology

   c We are all part of a system.

11 Which is the odd one out? Maturana says:

   a All behaviour is outcome driven

   b All our life experiences are encoded in our neurology

   c We have all the resources we need or can create them.

12 Which is the odd one out? Maslow and Rogers are the source of:

  (a) We have all the resources we need or can create them

  b We are all part of a system

  c The Map is not the Territory.

13 Which is the odd one out? Miller, Galanter and Pribram are the source of:

  (a) All behaviour is outcome driven

  b All behaviour is positively intended

  c We have all the resources we need, or can create them.

14 Which is the odd one out? Erickson is the source of:

  a The meaning of our communication is the response that we get

  (b) There is no such thing as a resistant person

  c There is no such thing as failure only feedback.

15 Which is the odd one out? Korzybski is the source of:

  a The Map is not the Territory

  (b) You cannot not communicate

  c Our Reality is what we believe to be true.

16 Which is the odd one out? W Ross Ashby is the source of:

  (a) Those who are the most flexible have the most influence

  b You cannot not communicate

  c There is no such thing as a resistant person.

Methodology

The Modelling Process

The Modelling Route Map

The following framework is the comprehensive model I devised to encapsulate the process of modelling and incorporate all the options and their permuations, available to a modeller. This thinking blows apart narrow approaches that may exist: myths about what modelling is and what modellers have to do. Here you can see that modelling is any activity which seeks to reveal the hidden structure of personalised experience.

Application Area	End User	Focus of Enquiry	Source(s) of Information	Types of Intervention	Types of Outcome
Personal Development	Third Party	Structure of Desired Behaviour (DB)	Self	Product and Process Models	Exploration / Identification of Structure
Therapy / Coaching	Self	Structure of Unwanted Behaviour (UB)	Exemplar	Modelling Methodologies	Remodelling of Structure
Consultancy / Training	Exemplar	Relationships between exemplar / DB / UB	Exemplars	Neurological Modelling	Model Construction
Others	Host Organisation		Literature and other media	Linguistic Modelling	
			Systems	Combination of above	Formal Acquisition

Quiz

1 Which statement is most accurate?

   a) There are many routes to achieving modelling outcomes

   b Modelling is about discovering the structure of excellence

   c You need three or more exemplars.

2 Which statement is most accurate? For successful modelling:

   a You need to apply a modelling methodology

   b You need three or more exemplars

   c) You focus on your end user.

3 Which statement is most accurate?

   a You can't model your own behaviour

   b You can use written sources

   c You need to see the behaviour in action.

4 Which statement is most accurate?

   a Modelling is not appropriate for the workplace

   b Modelling is the domain of therapy and coaching

   c Modelling can happens everywhere.

5 Which statement is the odd one out?

   a Unwanted behaviour can be a source of excellence

   b Modelling unwanted behaviour makes the behaviour worse

   c Unwanted behaviour reveals useful patterns.

6 Which statement is the odd one out?

   a End users can be known or unknown

   b You the modeller can be the end user

   c The exemplar only serves another end user.

7 Which statement is the odd one out?

   a Modelling is primarily concerned with individuals' behaviour

   b Systems created by people are outside of the domain of modelling

   c Any configuration of elements provides patterns to be modelled.

8 Which statement is the odd one out?

   a Modelling requires the ability to replicate behaviour in another

   b Modelling generates increased awareness

   c Modelling leads to the creation of techniques.

9 Which is correct?

   a Modelling can be applied anywhere

   b Only where there is dysfunction

   c Only where there is excellence.

10 Which is correct?

   a Acquisition has to be part of the modelling process

   b The modeller is the first acquirer

   c Acquisition has to replicate the exemplar's behaviour.

Plot the Route

The modeller has lots of choice available regarding the nature of their particular modelling activity. With this Route Map, the modeller can pre-determine the choices they want to make, whilst evaluating the additional options to draw on.

Scenario 1

You want to find out how someone is able to let go the need for certainty and become safely unsafe. Whilst you are aware there are times when you have overcome your default of timidity, when your desire to find out was so great, you feel there was more to it than that. You don't have access to any exemplars who have this confidence in the way you wanted. You have no desire to model the foolhardy, so you turn your attention to the writings of explorers and extreme sports enthusiasts who actively seek the thrill of being 'unsafe'. You want to find out what they have to believe to allow them to behave the way they do, consistently through time. You want to know how they approach 'danger'. You want to know what is important to them. Using the Neurological Levels, you tuck your information away in the awaiting sorting boxes. In the process you naturally notice where the differences lie, and what it might be like thinking, feeling or behaving like they do. You begin to get a glimpse into their worlds and how their energy is ignited. Over time, you find your own timidity has lessened as you intuitively draw on this new learning.

Application Area	End User	Focus of Enquiry	Source(s) of Information	Types of Intervention	Types of Outcome

Scenario 2

You are a consultant. Your client wants to unearth and rectify the poor communication and relationships between various bodies who are required to work collaboratively. Further funding for the organisation is dependent on improvement in this area. You gather the key players together with the intention of discovering how this system of poor communication drives itself. No one person has any greater authority in terms of insight over another. Whilst they are ostensibly discussing a topic, you observe the interactions that result. Through second positioning of individuals and the group as a whole, you notice the patterns as they emerge. You begin to plot the system, where energy flows and where it gets blocked.

After a significant period of time, you reflect back to them your findings which are real and undeniable, and invite them to come back with what needs to happen. You leave it to them to remodel the structure because they know the resources they have to work with.

Application Area	End User	Focus of Enquiry	Source(s) of Information	Types of Intervention	Types of Outcome

Scenario 3

You are aware of widespread interest in the nature of Happiness and seek to come up with a model which can usefully help others increase their levels of Happiness. You draw on your own experiences of Happiness, and discover the connection between the focus on time – past, present, and future – with associated language patterns. You test this with others and from this feedback you come up with a comprehensive model, which forms the basis of a workshop.

Application Area	End User	Focus of Enquiry	Source(s) of Information	Types of Intervention	Types of Outcome

Scenario 4

Your cllient seeks to alleviate her depression. Her marriage is in a poor state and has been for sometime. She knows if she manages to leave, her depression will lift, but because of her low energies she finds it hard to summon the will to do so. You explore with her the structure of her relationship, with her identifying key events from the start. Viewing these events on a screen up and in front of her, she begins to track the shifts in submodality configuration both for herself and for him. She can see how she has become shrunken and increasingly invisible, whille he has conversely become larger and and darker. She plays around with these constructions, matching earlier times and testing what fills her with confidence. With these new images in mind, she goes off to see what differences it makes to her responses to him.

Application Area	End User	Focus of Enquiry	Source(s) of Information	Types of Intervention	Types of Outcome

Scenario 5

You are working with a client who finds it hard to form good working relationships. She has been told at her annual appraisal that she needs to become more approachable with her staff and more collaborative with her colleagues. She finds this stressful and resents being told to become someone that she's not. She recognises that for the sake of her work, she needs to find a way of changing. She is single and says she would like to find someone but all her relationships are short lived when she finds fault with them. You invite her to explore the Wellbeing Model of Power, Control, Safety and Vulnerability, in which she has an initial strong response to Vulnerability. Working through the various elements and going to and fro, she gains insights into how she holds each element and how out of balance they have been. By the end of the session, she has achieved a state of calm and a solid grounding which she anchored and tested with future situations.

Application Area	End User	Focus of Enquiry	Source(s) of Information	Types of Intervention	Types of Outcome

Modelling Interventions

Quiz

1   Which statement is most accurate? An intervention is:

    a A written up technique

    b An act which generates change

    c A modelling interview.

2   Which statement is the odd one out? A NLP Product Technique:

    a Is usually devised by an unseen designer

    b Is designed to accommodate the needs of explorers

    c Is prescriptive.

3   Which statement is the odd one out? A NLP Process Technique:

    a Is usually devised by an unseen designer

    b Is designed to be responsive

    c Is prescriptive.

4   Which statement is the odd one out? A NLP Product Technique:

    a Is required to follow the set instructions

    b Is designed to be deliver a specific outcome

    c Is suitable for all explorers.

5   Which statement is the odd one out? An exemplar can benefit from:

    a Discovering how s/he does something well

    b Discovering patterns that generate unwanted behaviour

    c Discovering what is wrong with them.

6   Which statement is least accurate? A Modelling Methodology:

    a Is the most client focussed form of intervention

    b Is one approach to generating deepened awareness

    c Is a means of detecting patterns and structure.

7   Which statement is the odd one out? Techniques and Modelling Methodologies both:

    a Are predetermined

    b Are devised by unseen modellers

    c Serve the same purpose.

8   Which statement is the odd one out? A NLP Product Technique:

    a Can be adapted and added to

    b Can be used as a template for a different model

    c Is based on sequential models only.

9   Which statement is the odd one out? Modelling can be achieved through:

    a Using a modelling methodologies only

    b Applying of Neurological Frames

    c Applying of Linguistic Frames.

10 Which statement is the odd one out? Modelling can be achieved through:

    a Using a formal modelling methodologies only

    b Applying of Neurological Frames

    c Applying of Linguistic Frames.

Applying a Model

What Models do you know of and have possibly used that can reveal the structure, which within an individual is responsible for specific behaviour?

Neurological Modelling

List the range of neurological frames that you can use to model out the structure of internal experience.

1	4
2	5
3	6

Linguistic Modelling

List the range of language patterns you can use for modelling out the structure of internal experience.

1	6
2	7
3	8
4	9
5	10

20

Methodologies

We are blessed with a wide range of formal modelling methodologies at our disposal, ranging from the intuitive, through expressive and metaphorical, to cognitive. Taking these, in addition to the potential offered by neurological and linguistic modelling, and from the application of certain models, as modellers, we are spoilt for choice regarding the interventions we can take.

Quiz

1   Which statement is the odd one out?

   a   Modelling focuses on deep structure

   b   Modelling brings deep structure to the surface

   c   Modelling does not always result in cognitive awareness of patterns.

2   Which statement is the odd one out?

   a   Modelling can turn analogue experience into digital coding

   b   Digital coding generates cognition at surface structure

   c   Digital coding is the desired end result of modelling.

3   Which statement is the odd one out?

   a   The only proper form of modelling is Unconscious Uptake

   b   All modelling methodologies have a legitimacy

   c   Selection of methodology depends on modeller and exemplar.

4   Which is the odd one out? Methodologies are classified depending on:

   a   The level of language required by the exemplar

   b   The sophistication of the methodology and its skills

   c   The gap between the exemplars' representation and final coded model.

5   Which is the odd one out? The methodology originator:

   a   Needs to demonstrate the approach

   b   Doesn't need to provided a coded acquisition process

   c   Needs to be able to explain the rationale behind the approach.

6   Symbolic Modelling operates at:

   a   Deep Structure

   b   Mid Structure

   c   Surface Structure.

7   Somatic Modelling operates at:

   a   Deep Structure

   b   Mid Structure

   c   Surface Structure.

8   Analytical Modelling operates at:

   a   Deep Structure

   b   Mid Structure

   c   Surface Structure.

9   Punctuation Modelling operates at:

   a   Deep Structure

   b   Mid Structure

   c   Surface Structure.

10   Experiential Array Modelling operates at:

   a   Deep Structure

   b   Mid Structure

   c   Surface Structure.

Which Methodology Would You Choose?

Given the range of choice available to you, it is useful to be able to evaluate the relative merits of each modelling approach, so that you can select most appropriately to match the nature of the exemplar and the desired outcome.

Scenario 1

You want to model how your friend shuffles cards so well, but don't want to let on that you are emulating her. You want to keep your success a secret, until you can reveal your skill!

Scenario 2

You not only want to understand how your coachee perpetuates a particular bad habit, but you want him to know about it as well, so that he has the opportunity to self correct. You know that in other contexts this trait does not manifest itself.

Scenario 3

You want to discover the resources, required by a new team, to help them accelerate the problems of transition and enter into productive operation. You have been given an away-day to work with them. You want to use this opportunity to develop an overall model for Managing Transition Seamlessly.

Scenario 4

You want to help your client gain a sense of confidence in her future and strengthen her decision making abilities. She has had several previous counsellors and whilst she wants to improve, she is tired of talking about herself all the time. It hasn't seemed to make any difference. Whilst she uses kinaesthetic predicates, she seems to access her internal experience visually.

Scenario 5

You have a group of lively participants who are responsive to trying out something different. You have reached a place in your programme where the topic is 'Letting Go', and you want them to model out their own particular process in holding and letting go.

Scenario 6

You are about to introduce the subject of modelling to a new group. You want to provide a code congruent experience of learning about modelling, which offers the full process without requiring a preframe of the theory.

Relationship Skills

When working with exemplars as the source of your data, your abilities to manage the relationship directly contribute to your success.

Handling Relationship

Pitfalls and Antidotes

Example:

Exemplar has said many people have tried to find out his magic and none have succeeded. He doesn't think that your approach will work, but he's willing to give you 30 minutes of his time. He recognises the need to generate staff who are more productive and independent, so is interested to find out what you discover.

Guard against

- Putting yourself under time pressure

- Collude with his sense of unfathomability.

- Picking up the gauntlet to prove that NLP will work, and end up doing most of the work.

- Believing him when he says he wants others to be like him.

Antidotes

- **Be absolute prepared** in terms of equipment, materials and scoping framework – with a mindful eye on flexibility.

- **Pace** his sense of uniqueness and lead with everyone's behaviour is driven by an unique underpinning structure.

- **Spell out the benefits,** personally for him, as well as for his staff and his organisation.

- **Clarify his outcome** for his staff.

- **Be genuinely fascinated** whilst maintaining task focussed.

Scenario 1

This exemplar irritates you. She is a highly privieged young woman who has been given so much. She seems really arrogant, unware of her good fortune and dismissive of others. She finds it hard to answer your questions, often coming to a halt with 'Don't know', appearing confused and exasperated.

Guard Against

Antidote

Scenario 2

You are choosing to model out the unwanted behaviour. Through meta model questioning you are seeking to access the limiting beliefs which are driving your exemplar's behaviour. Your exemplar is looking increasingly uncomfortable, and the flow of his responses is slowing up, which you put down to the unfamiliarity of the territory you are exploring. You press on.

Guard Against

Antidote

Scenario 3

Exemplar has agreed to be part of your list of exemplars, and felt gratified that you had asked. However, she leads an erratic life, with shared child care arrangements with ex, a partner who works shifts, and she is a supply teacher. She had cancelled several appointments and so you arranged an evening meeting, which she also cancelled at the last minute. She has arrived late for the rearranged, rearranged session. You are up against a deadline yourself.

Guard Against

Antidote

Scenario 4

Your exemplar is your son's girlfriend, and she has been put forward for coaching by the organisation. She is highly ambitious and he is not, and they are currently going through a bad patch. You've had stories from your son who appears to be really upset, but have not spoken to her. She seems reluctant to speak freely with you.

Guard Against

Antidote

Scenario 5

Your exemplar is describing a family issue, involving her husband's family – in particular her brother-in-law – and how badly it is affecting her and her husband. She is estranged from her own family and relies heavily on all being well here. She feels the loss of her connection with her brother-in-law. Since nothing particularly serious seems to have happened, especially not to her, you are wondering what all the fuss is about.

Guard Against

Antidote

Scenario 6

Your exemplar has come to you to be rid of a flying phobia. You have allocated one hour, and after a short introduction, you take him through the standard Fast Phobia 'Cure'. By way of subsequent chat, he mentions issues about being an anxious car passenger and having problems at work, which you don't have time to go into.

Guard Against

Antidote

Scenario 7

You have identified three exemplars who have agreed to be interviewed or modelled by you. It took some time to identify and pin them down. You are aware of the time commitment they are offering. One of them is your line manager and you are anxious to acquit yourself well. Another is a friend, and another is someone you've been introduced to. You find that an element from your boss's information jars with your values. And the third exemplar has to cancel at short notice.

Guard Against

Antidote

Scenario 8

You have been given the fantastic opportunity to model a personal hero. You have decided to go for a particular modelling methodology since it is one that you are comfortable with and feel confident about using. However, your exemplar doesn't seem to want to follow your line of questioning. He seems to believe he knows what you need to know and goes about telling you. He definitely avoids answering questions that take him to unfamiliar places.

Guard Against

Antidote

Scenario 9

During your session with your exemplar, you noted that she waves her hands about a lot and uses lots of expressive facial gestures. She has particularly striking manicured nails and several expensive looking rings. She is carefully madeup with dominantly applied lipstick. To avoid being distracted by this effusive show, you focus on what she is saying and the patterns that are emerging, in line with her outcome.

Guard against

Antidotes

Scenario 10

This is your fourth exemplar. You have a pretty good idea of what the emierging model might be and you sense you are going through the motions here. In fact you realise that this exemplar deviates from the others and isn't really contributing anything of value.

Guard against

Antidotes

Scenario 11

You are thoroughly enjoying your session with this exemplar. You've hit it off well and he seems really into the process and is a pleasure to work with. His answers are seemingly honest and disarming, and he is fascinated by what your questions are bringing forth. He is entertaining and provides some fabulous anecdotes to illustrate what he is saying.

Guard against

Antidotes

Scenario 12

You are now in the position to construct your own original technique from the model you have created. You have spent a lot of time wondering what you are going to do. You are presenting your workshop around your findings in a couple of days time, and have just heard that the time allocated for it has been reduced to only three hours.

Guard against

Antidotes

Meta Messages

We can deliberately or unintentionally send out inexplicit messages, arising from our actions. These messages may help or hinder our efforts to establish a credible and effective relationship with others.

Exercise 1

What might a professional be saying if he or she:

Behaviour	Possible Intended Meta Message
	Possible Received Meta Message
Turns up late for sessions	
Favours one learner more than the others	
Wears smart expensive clothing	
Refers to own teachers and training events attended	
Listens attentively to questions	
Reads a novel whilst group is undertaking a set task	
Congruently admits not to know something	
Tells self deprecating stories about own learning experiences	

Exercise 2

Go second position to your customers and clients, and for each of the following identify the meta messages you are transmitting through your:

Marketing materials, website, logo, layout	
Venues, premises	
The way you handle enquiries and registrations	
Your personal appearance and style	

Working with Universal Patterns

Often you may find that your relationship with your exemplar has run into difficulties. You need to get the process flowing again, which requires you to go second position with your exemplar and identify where the differences between the two of you are lying, discovering the assumptions that you may have been making inadvertantly – or could be making.

This process requires you to establish Universal Statements which reflect your understanding of the exemplar's current reality and, through pacing these, demonstrate that you are starting from the exemplar's map. Traditionally, after three pacing statements you lead with one which takes you both in the direction you want to pursue. If it doesn't then you are back to pacing again, until you get movement. You may recognise that this pattern works well with reframes within Dilt's Sleight of Mouth, and Milton Model language.

Establishing or Re-establishing Rapport

Following the following scenarios, identify 3 universals and then provide a leading statement.

Worked example

This is a team of senior executive managers ,on an away day, looking at 'Implementing Cultural Change'.

Pace:

1   I know you are all very busy and I want to make sure I help to make this a really useful investment of your time.

2   Some of you may already have ideas about Cultural Change and how to bring it about,

3   Whilst understandably there may be others amongst you questioning the relevance of this initiative, given all the other demands placed on you, and the company at the moment.

Lead: This is why it is so important to tap into the wide range of thinking currently operating, so that we can use it to open up understanding, and generate buy-in for what is an essential next step in our continuing growth.

Scenario 1

This is your exemplar's first session with you. He has issues with Control. He has recently been seeing a CBT counsellor referred to by his GP. Already he has contradicted several things you have said.

Pace:

1

2

3

Lead:

Scenario 2

Your exemplar finds it really hard to talk about a certain subject and is constantly avoiding all reference to it.

Pace:

1

2

3

Lead:

Scenario 3

Your client, the Training Manager, has taken exception to something you have just said.

Pace:

1

2

3

Lead:

Scenario 4

Your Coaching exemplar is concerned that you will think she is stupid, and wrong to have the thoughts she has.

Pace:

1

2

3

Lead:

Scenario 5

Your Contracting Manager is raising questions about the effectiveness of the enquiry process to date.

Pace:

1

2

3

Lead:

Scenario 6

You have introduced an exercise requiring the participants to step into various spatial anchors, arranged on the floor. You have met resistance in some quarters.

Pace:

1

2

3

Lead:

Scenario 7

You want to book an hour of a senior manager's time to be an exemplar, and she is showing some reluctance regarding its usefulness.

Pace:

1

2

3

Lead:

Scenario 8

You have spent time with key senior supervisors, and are presenting your findings to the General Manager. He has become defensive and is unreceptive to hearing your evidence.

Pace:

1

2

3

Lead:

Working With Data

Thinking Logically

A significant contribution to being skilled at systemic thinking is the ability to be flexible when it comes to categorising and labelling information. The more types of information that you can contemplate, the more easily you will be able to spot similarities and detect patterns through isolating differences.

Exercise 1 – Identifying Logical Types

List as many Logical Type categories that you can think of – e.g.: function, composition, contribution.

Exercise 2 – Widening Thinking

What is this?

Referring to your range of Logical Types, come up with a minimum of 20 suggestions for the illustration below, viewing it at different scales, time and perspective.

1 A crack in the door	2	3
4	5	6
7	8	9
10	11	12
13	14	15
16	17	18
19	20	21
22	23	24
25	26	27
28	29	30

Exercise 3 – Widening Thinking

What is this?

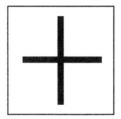

Now apply your thinking to this shape.

1	2	3
4	5	6
7	8	9
10	11	12
13	14	15
16	17	18
19	20	21
22	23	24
25	26	27
28	29	30

Pattern Detection

Exercise 1 – Party Games

Spot the patterns

1   I like yellow. I don't like red; I like green. I don't like road; I like jelly. I don't like fruit.

2   I like yellow. I don't like wood; I like wood. I don't like drains; I like drains. I don't like snow.

3   I like tree. I don't like grass; I like street light. I don't like pavement; I like statue. I don't like platform.

4   I like hands. I don't like gloves; I like letters. I don't like envelopes; I like hot water. I don't like hot water bottles.

5   I like ceilings. I don't like floors; I like skies. I don't like ground; I like hats. I don't like heads.

Exercise 2 – Cracking The Code

From the following data, work out your answer to the questions.

Question 1

= 26

= 34

What is 42?

Question 2

26 =   34 =

What is 23?

Exercise 3 – Ericksonian Riddles

Worked example

Question: What is the subject?

- a Wonder of the World

- a specimen of flora

- a genealogical framework

- a receiver of stolen goods

- a form of tennis

Answer:	A GARDEN
• a Wonder of the World	Great Wall of China
• a specimen of flora	Flower
• a genealogical framework	(Family) Tree
• a receiver of stolen goods	Fence
• a form of tennis	Lawn

Note: You couldn't have Hanging Gardens of Babylon because you can't include the thing of which it is a class.

You will find many more of these puzzles on The NLP Kitchen – www.nlpand.co.uk

Puzzle 1

What is the subject?

- a ravine

- a half dozen

- a petticoat

- a winged mammal

- a fruit container

Puzzle 2

What is the subject?

- paving stones

- a month of the year

- to be on the surface of water

- little army officers

- traditional Yorkshire music makers

Sorting Challenges

Exercise 1 – Finding Connections

When we are asked to deliberately seek similarities between apparently totally disparate things, it is amazing just where our mind can go to achieve this. We have to break free from our habitual associations and seek new ways of combining difference. This requires us to hold our certainty more lightly, and be open to new ideas that emerge within the process.

From the following list, select four to five items and identify what they have in common.

The British Commonwealth	A family	Space exploration
A sock drawer	A busy roundabout	A stapler
A jar of bubbles	The House of Commons	A balloon
A playground	A car manufacturing plant	A rare vase
A boutique	A heckler	A sense of shame
A child prodigy	A tree	A satellite dish
A football team	The Head Teacher	A National Park
A railway viaduct	A chimney pot	An index
Your digestive system	A compass	Swine Flu
A daffodil	A soft toy	The Tourism Industry
A bottle of water	A career	A Hollywood Star
A TV drama programme	An orchestral piece	A street light
The internet	A religious faith	Roof tiles
A holiday	A childhood memory	Teeth
Old age	A retail franchise	Telegraph wires
Getting drunk	Painting an oil painting	Tenants
Designing a building	Singing in a choir	Combustion engine

Exercise 2 – Scoping

Imagine the following items were in a bag. Take them out and come up with 10 different categories you could sort them into.

Lingerie	Apple	Book	Paper clip
Risotto	Banana	**Box**	**Paper bag**
Cardigan	RULER	Aspirin packet	Quorn
Slippers	Pencil	JACKET	Zip
Chiffon Scarf	Screwdriver	**Tara masala**	Buttons
ORANGE	Hammer	String	WASHER

Exercise 3

Group the following items into a coherent pattern. (You may like to write the roles onto separate bits of paper so you can move them around and work through various configurations)

Shop Assistant	Archaeologist	Tour Guide
Impresario	Engineer	Baker
Farmer	Composer	Geologist
Museum Curator	Constructor	Conductor

Exercise 4

Here's an interesting challenge for you, to practise your thinking on structure. Sort these items into sets of three, and state the structure you think links them.

- A strawberry cream chocolate
- A game of Jenga – where you pull bricks out of a pile
- A busy motorway interchange
- Blowing up a balloon
- A complex country dance
- A tangled ball of string
- A Shakespearian Play

- Weighing sugar accurately
- Disabled parking spaces
- A soft boiled egg
- A shopping queue
- An active volcano
- A highly attractive physicist
- Dress code
- A lively sports car

				The Shared Structure
1 e.g.	A busy motorway interchange	A complex country dance	A tangled ball of string	There is always a clear pathway to follow
2				
3				
4				
5				

Exercise 5

What does all of this represent?

Beautiful hands

Likes banter

Logical   5'7'-6'   Emotional nature

Kind

Style

Considerate   **Social Behaviour**   Stylish

Likes variety

Casual   Intuitive

Good conversationalist

Medium   Funny   Calm
Weight   Enjoys
                people

Smart

Quick witted   Nice eyes

Spends money
thoughtfully   Social Behaviour   Easy going   Looks

Love Making

Caring

Adventurous   Well read

Appearance

Personal Attributes

Rational   Likes   Holds his
                quality   **Mind**   ground

Unselfish

Lovely smile

Passionate   Fashionable

Gathering Information

Asking Questions

You gather information through your sensory acuity, and through your ability to ask precise and targeted questions. Being able to ask questions that generate volumes of quality information, quickens the elicitation process and maintains relationship with your source. The fewer questions the better.

Hitting The Target

Sometimes we need to find a different way of saying something, yet still meet our outcome. identify the outcome and come up with 5 different questions that could all serve to gain this outcome.

Worked example

What's in it for you to keep doing this?

Outcome: To get to the Secondary Gain

1   What are you getting from doing this?

2   What is this giving you?

3   What need is this behaviour meeting?

4   What would you lose if you stopped doing this?

5   Who wouldn't you be if you stopped doing this?

---

1   What would you rather have?

Outcome

1

2

3

4

5

2   What's stopping you from doing this?

Outcome

1

2

3

4

5

3   What has to be true for this to be happening?

Outcome

1

2

3

4

5

4   What do you fear might happen?

Outcome

1

2

3

4

5

5   **What is important to you at the moment?**

Outcome

1

2

3

4

5

Finding the Question

We are always at choice regarding the question we frame and select to use. Some will gather shedloads of information and awareness; others will demand a swift follow-on question because of limited yield. Developing the ability to judge which question to ask will bring the greatest dividend and add to the elegance of your performance.

Here are some scenarios coming from a Therapy/Coaching world. The same principles apply in Business and Education contexts. In fact, if you really want to improve, record your interactions and note the questions you ask and the quality of the responses you gain.

For those unproductive questions, come up with what else you could have asked in that moment which would have harvested better results.

Worked Example

Rank the questions in order of appropriateness and give your reasons for your answer.

Worked example

You have become confused. Your exemplar was one minute talking about a frustrating incident when she was in a public meeting and switched quickly to an incident with one of her children where she had become upset. You have been pursuing the theme of creativity and her ability to discover creative opportunities. You previously had asked her 'When are you at your most creative?' and she had given examples of being on holiday in a remote cottage, and a time when she and a colleague were thrashing out an outline for a TV series.

1   How did your colleague activate your creativity?

2   What is the connection between the time in the cottage and working with your colleague, and the public meeting and that time with the children?

3   How do these events relate to creativity?

4   How does frustration affect your creativity?

5   What was the connection between the public meeting and that incident with your children?

Rank		Reason
1	Q 2	When confused, chunk up. This relevancy check serves to draw her attention to her train of thought, and reveal her own internal processing which may or may not be to do with creativity. It might be to do with doubt, or conditions required for creativity, or something else entirely. The question covers no presupposition other than possible connection. It also serves as a backtrack frame.
2	Q 3	This is a useful chunk up to provide an overview out of the specifics. This question does presuppose a link to creativity, or else you have usefully created such a link. You have missed the backtrack opportunity, and she may not have included all the events within her TDS (transderivational search) that she could have.
3	Q 4	You are still maintaining focus on creativity, which is your outcome, and you are seeking a connection between state and creativity. This is a narrow specific link which may or may not indicate a pattern. It might be that you have to chunk up after this question.
4	Q 5	You have gone for recency and sought to explore her immediate thinking patterns. What will this information now give you? Where would you need to go next?
5	Q 1	You have gone back to the last known point of discussing creativity. Yet this is such a small chunk piece of information, you will still be in the fog of the bigger picture.

Scenario 1

Your client has spent the last ten minutes going over old ground, some familiar and some in greater detail. He says he is seeking self confidence and a sense of purpose and focus, yet every time you seek to steer him to look to the future, he goes off on another tangent. This is your third session and you seem to be getting nowhere.

1 What would happen if you achieved self confidence, a sense of purpose and focus?

2 What do you fear you might lose if you achieved self confidence, a sense of purpose and focus?

3 You may have noticed whenever I attempt to direct your attention to future events, you divert elsewhere. How familiar is this pattern of yours generally?

4 You have great confidence in covering known experience. What stops you from exploring new ground?

5 I'm finding this really difficult. You say you want to move forwards and gain a sense of purpose, yet you constantly seem to want to talk about what has been. What would you do now, if you were me?

Rank		Reason
1	Q	
2	Q	
3	Q	
4	Q	
5	Q	

Scenario 3

Your client has come to you with her real fear of public speaking. She becomes phobic, sweats, flushes and is incapable of speech. In her new role, she is required to present at meetings and offer training presentations. Previously she has managed to get cover, but she believes she is in danger of being demoted.

1 What do you think is the positive intention of the Part that is responsible for your phobic response?

2 When have you not responded as severely as you might have expected, or didn't have an adverse response at all?

3 What would it be like to step into the shoes of someone who presents in the way that you admire?

4 How else might you be protected when you become publicly visible, so that you don't have to have that old phobic response?

5 What do you think is stopping you?

Rank		Reason
1	Q	
2	Q	
3	Q	
4	Q	
5	Q	

Scenario 4

Your client is deeply upset. She is suffering from a loss of self and fears that she is in need of deep and sustained therapy. She is the mother of a 6 month old boy and has asked that her mother doesn't visit. She is estranged from her father. She is in a loving relationship, although not married.

She has a business 'partner' whom she respects and admires. This partner has been strongly suggesting that the business failings are down to your client's chaotic unresolved relationship with her parents. The partner has also deeply criticised your client's skills and ability to bring in business. It appears that your client is fully responsible for bringing in all the business and last year there was a turnover of £¼ M. Your client is meant to be receiving 20% of profits but has so far only received her delivery rate.

1   What is happening between you and your parents at the moment?

2   You have a partner who is a manipulative, lazy, deceitful bully. What's *your* problem?

3   How much do you think you are contributing to the non-functioning of the business?

4   How might your business partner be projecting her own stuff at you?

5   How might your current response be down to postnatal depression?

Rank		Reason
1	Q	
2	Q	
3	Q	
4	Q	
5	Q	

Meta Model

Major on at least becoming absolutely fluent with Meta Model. This is a gift for anyone who wants to retrieve deep structure information, painlessly and efficiently. This is your challenge. Take it and your practice will improve through the roof!

Quiz

1   The source of a generalised rule is retrieved through asking the following type of question:

   a Simple Deletion

   b Modal Operator of Necessity

   c Lost Performatives.

2   The limitation affecting a behaviour is retrieved through asking the following type of question:

   a Modal Operator of Probability

   b Complex Equivalence

   c Referential Index.

3   The meaning the speaker is putting onto something is retrieved through asking the following type of question:

   a Complex Equivalence

   b Cause and Effect

   c Mindreading.

4   The subject of the statement is retrieved through asking the following type of question:

   a Simple Deletion

   b Unspecified Verb

   c Unspecified Referential Index.

5   The consequences of an action are retrieved through asking the following type of question:

   a Complex Equivalence

   b Cause and Effect

   c Mindreading.

6   The process involved in an action are retrieved through asking the following type of question:

   a Complex Equivalence

   b Unspecified Verb

   c Nominalisation.

7   The action involved in an event is retrieved through asking the following type of question:

   a Lost Performatives

   b Unspecified Verb

   c Nominalisation.

8   The generalised conclusion within a statement is retrieved through asking the following type of question:

   a Cause and Effect

   b Unspecified Verb

   c Nominalisation.

9   The projection of thought is retrieved through asking the following type of question:

   a Modal Operator of Necessity

   b Universal Quantifier

   c Mindreading.

Hidden Meta Model Patterns

We aren't always handed easily recognisable 'can't's' and 'should's'. We need to be able to detect each pattern, even when it is disguised in unfamiliar language. Unless we really understand the nature of the pattern, we won't be able to spot it if hidden in other words or phrases, which means we will be missing lots of important clues offered by the explorer.

Here are some examples of how each pattern could be expressed in everyday language.

• Modal Operator of Possibility	impossible, difficult,
• Modal Operator of Necessity	essential, imperative,
• Universal Quantifiers	continuously, constantly,
• Lost Performatives	People who … You find that…
• Mind Reading	You're bound to … They won't want to …
• Cause and Effect	undesirable consequences, inevitable
• Complex Equivalence	implies, denotes,

Now come up with 5 -10 different ways each of these patterns could be expressed.

Meta Model Pattern	Different ways it can be expressed
Modal Operator of Necessity	
Modal Operator of Probability	

The Bumper Bundle Companion Exercises

Universal Quantifier	
Lost Performative	
Mind Reading	
Cause and Effect	
Complex Equivalence	

What to Go For

Elegance witth Meta Model is knowing what to pursue and what to leave alone. First of all you need to notice the patterns as they arise and determine their significance before deciding which door to go in through.

However, instead of diving in immediately, it is worthwhile evaluating the informtion you are spotting within the wider context of what you are being offered. Deciding where the nuggets of information lie – those which will move understanding forwards – and ignoring those patterns which will yield little, will help you to maintain relationship and gather quality information with the minimum disruption.

The following examples offer you first of all an isolated statement, which you are asked to deconstruct into its meta model patterns. Then you are asked to decide what to pursue once you are given the wider context.

Code for the patterns

SD: Simple Deletion

CD: Comparative Deletion

LRI: Lack of Referential Index

UV: Unspecified Verb

N: Nominalisation

MOP: Modal Operator of Possibility

MON: Modal Operator of Necessity

U: Universal

LP: Lost Performative

MR: Mindreading

CE: Cause and Effect

CEQ: Complex Equivalence

Worked example

It is impossible to get through to them. They are typical managers and don't listen.
MOP   UV   SD   LRI   U   LP   CEQ
I have tried and tried telling them. I've phoned and left messages. Emailed. I've even waylaid one of the managers in the corridor. It's impossible to get through to them. They are typical managers and don't listen. I suspect it is personal and they won't take it from a woman.
Ah hah! By holding back and allowing the speaker to carry on, you now have discovered an interesting Mind Reading Pattern, which could have a great influence on the situation.

The Bumper Bundle Companion Exercises

Example 1

> I always end up badly in negotiations. I've become really nervous and now my reputation has
>
> suffered.

> I don't have the killer instinct that this job seems to demand. I always end up badly in negotiations. I've become really nervous and now my reputation has suffered. But I don't want to be one of those hardened, screw 'em type of guys. I can't see why we can't go for a win:win outcome.

Example 2

> This is blissful! Everyone should love this, or else they have no soul!

> I can't stand those people who turn their nose up at a bit of luxury and make out that they are somehow superior. This is blissful! Everyone should love this, or else they have no soul!

Example 3

That suggestion is out of the question. It's totally disrespectful to expect us to respond in this

manner! I feel quite insulted.

We have provided them with all the information and now they are suggesting that we now become part of a tendering process. That suggestion is out of the question. It's totally disrespectful to expect us to respond in this manner! I feel quite insulted. I have a good mind to contact the CEO tell her that we are withdrawing from the whole process.

Example 4

I feel a failure. I should have done more to keep my marriage alive.

I feel a failure. I should have done more to keep my marriage alive. My husband says it is nothing to do with me; just that he wants different things. He even said that he knew he shouldn't have married me at the time! But there must be something wrong with me, that I'm not enough for him.

Frames and Reframes

Outcome Frame

It is important that you are fully aware of the purpose of each of these components, within the Outcome Frame: otherwise you may be tempted to overlook, or discount, those that don't make an impact on you, or which are unfamiliar.

It is also important that you can explain the thinking behind your questions to your explorer, to help them understand the process they are going through.

Outcome Element	Purpose
1 Positive Statement	
2 Value	
3 Context	
4 Evidence	
5 Contribution	

6 Resources	
7 Ecology	
8 Future Pace	

Working with the Outcome Frame

Often we are given much of the information we need to construct a well formed outcome, without having to go through the full procedure. The trick is noticing what we've been given. The following tasks invite you to spot what has been included and what you now need to go for.

Task 1

'I really hope it happens this time. It would be the break I've always wanted after all my hard work. It would make all the setbacks worthwhile. My Dad would be so proud of me, telling all his mates and taking all the credit!'

• Which components have you been given?

• What might you usefully explore now?

Task 2

'I want to achieve £100,000 per annum turnover in the next year starting from January. I've networked, blogged, optimized my website, spoken to lots of people. Getting this would mean I am somebody, and people would have to sit up and listen. I promised myself a year ago that this would happen. I wrote out the outcome, did the full process – but it hasn't happened yet.'

• Which components have you been given?

• What might you usefully explore now?

Task 3

'I'm 38 and I just feel that there is more out there for me. My kids are in secondary school and will soon be ready to be off doing their own thing. Mike is well established in his career and seems to be enjoying himself. I just feel so unfulfilled. I want to know what I will be doing something worthwhile by the time I reach 40.'

• Which components have you been given?

• What might you usefully explore now?

Task 4

'I want a good Law Degree. I know that there is a lot of work involved and that I must balance out studying with keeping my cycling alive. Can't get too bogged down. It will be great walking across the platform, cap and gown, receiving my degree. It's a long way off, so you can't get too excited about it at the moment can you? I mean it is sort of academic, pun unintended, isn't it?'

• Which components have you been given?

• What might you usefully explore now?

Obscure Outcomes

Often supposed outcomes are sabotaged by what might be lost in the achieving of them. This is often the reason for lack of success, held at an unconscious level. Revealing this can be a complete surprise for the individual, certainly in the face of all their apparent effort. Discovering the Secondary Gain derived from being unsuccessful can then be addressed by identifying the Positive Intention of holding that Secondary Gain.

Once the Positive Intention can be met in another way, then the individual may be predisposed to letting go of the Secondary Gain.

Worked example

Action	What is my Secondary Gain?	What is my Positive Intention?
Having a bad back	Receiving physical attention from the another person (physio)	To feel a connection with another

The Bumper Bundle Companion Exercises

Exercise

Action	What is my Secondary Gain?	What is my Positive Intention?
Getting poor results at college		
Turning down invitations to go on foreign holidays		
Eating too much		
Not settling down into a permanent relationship		

Come up with two of your own

PRO Statements

Often a presented Outcome masquerades as a Remedy: a statement which still holds part of the Problem.

To achieve well-formedness, these are the questions you offer in response to the explorer's statements with the aim of developing a discrete outcome.

PROBLEM	And what would you like to have happen, when [Problem]?	
REMEDY	And when [Remedy] then what happens?	
OUTCOME	And when you have X [the Outcome] would you want it?	

P R or O	Which is which?	Question
	I am motivated and enthusiastic.	
	We want to be recognised.	
	I want to be more effective.	
	I want to feel optimistic.	
	We want to win the Best Team Award.	
	I want to be less negative.	
	I am a good decision maker.	
	We are overlooked.	
	I do the same things time and again.	

The Bumper Bundle Companion Exercises

General Frames

As If, Relevancy Challenge, Constrast, Backtrack, are all Linguistic Frames, as a means of clarifying statements and framing context.

Which frame would you use when your explorer:

Situation	Frame
1 is confused and doesn't trust his thinking.	
2 has at least two options both of which seem fairly attractive.	
3 has just gone through a fairly rambling account, and has paused for breath.	
4 has gone off on a tangent, after you asked a specific meta model question.	
5 keeps saying 'I don't know' when you are asking 'Whereabouts is that feeling?'	
6 has offered four possible causal outcomes based on Lost Performatives and Mind Readings.	
7 has mentioned an ex partner frequently when discussing her current relationship?	
8 has begun to tell a story when you've asked 'What would you like to have happen?'	
9 has introduced two seemingly disconnected stories, considering the subject that you were talking about.	
10 finds it difficult to say what he thinks the consequences might be.	

Integration

Deconstructing Language

To claim linguistic mastery, you need to be able to explain how language achieves the effect it does, and how its construction contributes directly to this. This way, you will be able to quickly detect the impact of the words you are hearing, and be able to construct precise wording to meet your own outcomes directly with the minimum of fuss. This is the mark of elegance.

Previous exercises have explored various aspects of linguistic construction. This section brings it all together, and asks for your accountability to your linguistic craft.

You are given a series of three sets of questions. These questions were used as a pre-frame at the start of various days on a training programme: as a means of reviewing the previous day's activities and learning; an opportunity to test understanding of language use; and for setting filters for the day to come.

The Bumper Bundle Companion Exercises

Worked example 1

- What have you been most proud of?
- What has this given you now?
- How can this make a difference to you this weekend?

Presuppositions	Q1 Not only has there been things to make the learner proud, but there have been at least 3 or more.
	Q1 Being proud of yourself and/or your behaviours gives you something additional. The tense 'has given' suggests that this meta awareness has already happened.
	Q3 These actions, or its effects can make a difference within the timeframe of the weekend.
Timeframe	Q1 There is a deletion here. The reference to this weekend is suggesting the intervening period since the previous weekend. Ideally 'since the previous weekend?' should be added. This may well have been stated at the point of delivery.
	Q2 The use of 'now' brings attention into this moment.
	Q3 Takes attention into the near future of the next four days.
Transderivational Search	Reference experiences of pride in relation to self and actions. Evaluation of these moments as being worthy of pride.
Meta Model	Q3 Modal Operator of Possibility – use of 'can' reduces options and is directive. If marked out tonally then there is an embedded suggestion.
Milton Model	Q3 Modal Operator of Possibility – use of 'can', if marked out tonally, provides an embedded suggestion.
Neurological Level	Values: Pride. Capability: Ability to act on awareness to make a difference.
Perspective	Use of 'this' in Q2 and twice in Q3 strengthens association.
Meta Message	Being proud is a good thing. The cause of our pride can contribute to our performance. Everyone has permission to blow their own trumpet.
Outcome	To declare your pride in yourself. To feel good about yourself as a learner.

Worked example 2

- Who are you now that you weren't expressing before?

- What animal would represent before and now?

- What might you want it to be?

Presuppositions	Q1	New personal aspects are now emerging. Aspects of oneself are expressed. That there has been a shift.
	Q2	Animals have characteristics which can metaphorically sum up our behaviours. There is a before and a now.
	Q3	That there is still development to come.
Timeframe	Q1	Viewing the passage of time from before to now, in an unspecified timeframe.
	Q2	Same as above.
	Q3	Takes attention into unspecified future.
Transderivational Search		Previous limitations and constraints on personality within the learning context. Awareness of what was missing, and what is still missing. Future goal.
Meta Model	Q2	Modal Operator of Possibility – use of 'would' offers choice.
	Q3	Modal Operator of Possibility – use of 'might' makes it more optional.
Neurological Level		Identity – 'are you' represented in use of metaphor.
Perspective		2nd positioning an animal.
Meta Message		Learning brings change and they will have changed. There is always room for further development. The Learner has a choice about who they can become.
Desired Outcome		To realise the continuum of development and self determination.

Exercise 1

- What was surprising you about your performance?
- How did you manage that?
- What beliefs and values were influencing your decision-making?

Presuppositions	
Timeframe	
Transderivational Search	
Meta Model	
Neurological Level	
Perspective	
Meta Message	
Desired Outcome	

Exercise 2

- What is continually delighting you?
- What does this tell you about your Purpose?
- What will be the significance of that?

Presuppositions	
Timeframe	
Transderivational Search	
Meta Model	
Neurological Level	
Perspective	
Meta Message	
Desired Outcome	

Exercise 3

- What has been drawing your attention and interest?
- How might this compare with the experiences of others?
- What could this say about you as a Learner?

Presuppositions	
Timeframe	
Transderivational Search	
Meta Model	
Neurological Level	
Perspective	
Meta Message	
Desired Outcome	

Exercise 4

- Knowing what you know now, and having the skills you can now draw on, how will this assist your learning today?

- And how else?

Presuppositions	
Timeframe	
Transderivational Search	
Meta Model	
Neurological Level	
Perspective	
Meta Message	
Desired Outcome	

Exercise 5

- What is guaranteed to inspire you as a learner?
- What does this say about you?
- How does this affect your relationship with learning?

Presuppositions	
Timeframe	
Transderivational Search	
Meta Model	
Neurological Level	
Perspective	
Meta Message	
Desired Outcome	

Exercise 6

- What have you been noticing about your learning?

- What would you rather have?

- How will this have been of more benefit to you and others?

Presuppositions	
Timeframe	
Transderivational Search	
Meta Model	
Neurological Level	
Perspective	
Meta Message	
Desired Outcome	

Exercise 7

- How have you been restricting your learning?
- How has this been serving you?
- How might others have described that?

Presuppositions	
Timeframe	
Transderivational Search	
Meta Model	
Neurological Level	
Perspective	
Meta Message	
Desired Outcome	

Exercise 8

- What unexpected success did you have?

- How did you make this happen?

- How will this be important in your everyday work?

Presuppositions	
Timeframe	
Transderivational Search	
Meta Model	
Neurological Level	
Perspective	
Meta Message	
Desired Outcome	

Technology

Techniques

The Nature of Techniques

Selection of Techniques

When you select a technique to offer to your client, you need to have a clear understanding of the reasons for its selection. This will prevent you from just picking a favourite, or your flavour of the month, or one you are seeking to practice, or one you've just learnt.

Think back to the last formal technique that you selected to use when working with an explorer. Write down your comments regarding your choice against each of the following considerations.

The Technique:	
Your Outcome What did you want to achieve? Did you?	
Structure of the Problem How did the selection pace the needs of the explorer?	

Readiness to Explore How much information had you gathered which led to this selection?	
Your Skill Levels How congruent were you regarding your abilities to deliver this technique?	
Efficiency and Elegance How deep was the rapport throughout the process? How effective were you taking the minimum amount of time required?	
Recency How often do you select this technique? When did you first learn it?	
Flexibility How much did you deviate from the normal approach, and why?	

Purpose of the Common Techniques

Unless you fully understand the intended outcome of each technique, you will not be able to select with precision. It is important not only to be conversant with the technique's purpose, you also need to know when you have reached completion – i.e. what is the evidence that you are calibrating.

For the following techniques that are found in the syllabus of most Practitioner trainings, identify the intended outcome of each, and what calibration evidence are you requiring before you exit your TOTE?

	Purpose	Calibration Evidence
6 Step Reframe		
Change Personal History		
Circle of Excellence		
Disney Strategy		
Meta Mirror		

Neurological Level Alignment		
New Behaviour Generator		
Phobia 'Cure'		
SCORE		
Swish		
Timeline Alignment		
Visual Squash		

Components within a Technique

Designing an original technique is really easy, once you are clear about the four components which are required to bring a digital model back to analogue experience.

Name the four components that make a technique.

Skills for Technique Delivery

The following skills are all involved in working with an explorer and delivery a technique effectively, efficiently and hopefully elegantly. Some of these skills you are comfortable with; some you may know you need to practise further.

To increase your motivation to continually improve your skills-set, it helps to have a clear understanding why each skill is important and where it fits in with the overall tradecraft.

Listing of skills

- Linguistic Delivery
- Second Positioning
- Responding to Own Incongruence
- Paying Attention to Ecology

- Sensory Acuity
- Maintaining Rapport
- Overcoming Resistance
- Managing Time
- Being Flexible
- Managing Space

- Positioning
- Resourcing
- Multiple Attending
- Managing Process
- Anchoring and Marking Out
- Sponsoring

Select a skill and identify its importance

	Skill	Its importance
1		
2		
3		
4		
5		
6		

7		
8		
9		
10		
11		
12		
13		
14		
15		
16		

Logistics of Time

Knowing the usual amount of time required to deliver a technique is essential for the appropriate selection of a technique. However other factors can influence the time a process takes. Time management requires high levels of flexibility on your part.

Identify which of the following factors influence the time required to perform a technique.

	Influences on Time	Yes	No
1	The complexity of the process.		
2	The skill of the practitioner.		
3	The ability of the explorer to access their unconscious mind.		
4	The size of the room.		
5	The seriousness of the problem.		
6	The nature of the problem.		
7	The level of preframe offered.		
8	The chunk size of the explorer's processing.		
9	The compatibility of the technique with the explorer.		
10	Unexpected developments.		
11	The frequency that this technique is selected.		
12	Deviation from the established process.		
13	The level of content offered by the explorer.		
14	The delivery method selected.		
15	Omission of certain elements within the technique.		
16	The physical stamina of the explorer.		
17	The past history of the explorer.		
18	Time pressures on explorer and on the practitioner.		

Selection of Interventions

Picking the best technique to generate the agreed outcome is the mark of good practitioner. At the same time, a technique will always let you down, so you are well served if you have a back up, up your sleeve.

Read through the following scenarios and work out what you think might be the best technique to use as an intervention – or not. You will need to be clear of your own outcome, and the evidence that you seek.

Scenario 1 – Jane

Jane is a highly competent supervisor, who is ripe for promotion, but who doesn't put her name forward for posts that she could easily secure. In conversation, she made reference to making presentations and how she hates them. Her last awful experience was on a training course and she was landed with presenting her group's findings. Even though it was merely one flipchart, her mouth went dry, she flushed up, she talked in a monotone, and every molecule of her body screamed 'Get me out of here!' She believes that if she gets promoted to a higher managerial position, she will have to make presentations regularly, and there is no way she wants to put herself through that. She would like to be promoted, and she would like to be rid of this fear.

Scenario 2 – Mike

Mike has just come out of his staff appraisal with his new Line Manager. He is oscillating between rage and wretchedness. From the day this woman arrived, she seemed to pick on him, belittling him in meetings, demanding reports to be rewritten, overlooking him for inclusion in a project involving his area of work. Inevitably his work began to suffer, and his confidence evaporate. In this most recent encounter, she systematically stripped him of any sense of self-belief where his work is concerned, ending up suggesting that he might consider looking elsewhere. He is left feeling totally impotent and incapable of standing up for himself. He would like to find a response to this bullying, but from an early age he has never been able to handle conflict.

Scenario 3 – Asif

Asif is in two minds about going for a new job. He knows it will mean more exposure and great opportunities for interesting projects, and the increased money would certainly be appreciated. At the same time, it would mean leaving his family home and setting up in his own flat. He doesn't want to upset his family, or be seen to be disloyal, yet he really wants the chance to learn more and show people what he can do. He would like to find a way to handle his parents and make them feel happy about his career progression.

Scenario 4 – Honour

Honour seems to be perpetually anxious, worrying over everything – her family, her husband, his job, her parents. She is now suffering from skin rashes and high blood pressure. The doctor is suggesting putting her on mild tranquilisers but she is reluctant to 'start taking pills' because she worries that she'll become addicted. Her family accept this saying she's always been like this, but as her own family is growing up, she is worried that she will never lead a normal life and that she will push everyone away. She would like to have a positive view of the future and feel much calmer.

Technique Components

Models

All methodologies have the potential to yield a digital coded model, which packages the dynamics of the behaviour modelled. Remember, however, that this is not an automatic requirement of the modelling process. Having an understanding of the types of models available to you, as a modeller, allows you more choice and direction when it comes to creating a model of your own. And then when it comes to constructing an original technique, I am suggesting that models form the basis of any technique. Once these have been identified, the practitioner can then decide the delivery method and neurological and linguistic frames.

Therefore it is important that you have clarity regarding the nature and function of a model.

Quiz

1 Which is the odd one out? An model seeks to:

  a Be a money spinner

  b Simplify a complex process

  c Aid navigation through a process.

2 Which statement is not accurate? A model seeks to:

  a Replicate exemplar's behaviour exactly

  b Provide the acquirer's description of the exemplar's behaviour

  c Provide behaviour in the same class of behaviour as the exemplar.

3 Which statement is not accurate? A model seeks to:

  a Expand awareness of the exemplar

  b Expand awareness of the acquirer

  c Expand awareness of modelling.

4 Which statement is accurate? For modelling purposes a Model is:

  a The Exemplar

  b The Exemplar's internal structure

  c The model produced by the modeller.

5 Which statement is correct? A Model needs to meet the following criteria:

  a Coherence, accessibility, aesthetics

  b Simplicity, accessibility, accuracy

  c Effectiveness, simplicity, coherence

6 Which statement is correct? A Model needs to meet the following criteria:

  a Aesthetics, accuracy, accessibility

  b Effectiveness, efficiency, elegance

  c Coherence, simplicity, accessibility.

7 Which statement is incorrect? A model can be:

  a A Table of Contents

  b A painting

  c A stone.

8 Which statement is incorrect? A model can be:

  a A fork

  b A strategy

  c A set of bullet points.

9 Which statement is correct? According to Burgess's Classification, there are:

a Natural and Constructed Models

b Natural, Idiosyncratic and Constructed Models

c Natural, Idiosyncratic, Generic and Constructed Models.

10 Which statement is incorrect? A Natural Model can be:

a The basis for a technique

b The basis for a modelling methodology

c The basis for a linguistic frame.

11 Which statement is incorrect? Examples of Natural Models are:

a Diagrams, Tables, Submodalities

b Submodalities, images, metaphors

c Perspectives, sounds, Parts.

12 Which statement is inaccurate? Idiosyncratic Models are:

a A generalised coded description from multiple sources

b An uncoded description from one source

c A unique description which can become a coded model.

13 Which statement is accurate? Examples of Idiosyncratic Models are:

a Illustrations, diagram, descriptions

b Sequential, hierarchical, simultaneous formats

c Diagrams, metaphors and tables.

14 Which statement is inaccurate? Constructed Models:

a Are fully coded descriptions

b Are the constructs of the modeller

c Are found naturally within everyone.

15 Which statement is accurate? Examples of Constructed Models are:

a Sequential, Simultaneous, Tabular

b Sequential, Iterative, Diagrammatic

c Illustrative, Hierarchical, Sounds.

The Bumper Bundle Companion Exercises

Labelling The Elements

For models to work, they need to be labelled precisely.   Here are three models, whose elements have been deliberately labelled badly. Identify what is wrong with each of them and identify the accepted model.

1	Critic, Creator, Planner, Dreamer	
2	Dreamlike, Planning, Criticism	
3	Look Up, To Do List, Criticism	
4	Be receptive, Dream, Have Ideas; Receive ideas, Identify resources, Make plans; Evaluate plans, Find problems, Ask questions	
Model 1: Accepted labelling		
5	Powerful, Controlling, Safely, Vulnerability	
6	Impotent, Over controlled, Unsafe, Impregnable	
7	Powerless, Controlled, Safety, Vulnerability	
Model 2: Accepted labelling		
8	Tenderness, Fierce, Playfulness	
9	Tender, Fiercely, Playing	
10	The Queen, The King, The Jester	
Model 3: Accepted labelling		

Name the Types of Models

Knowing the options available to you, in terms of the type of model you create, helps you make decisions about how you manipulate the data you've been gathering.

Here you are offered a range of models of various types. Identify the category of each model.

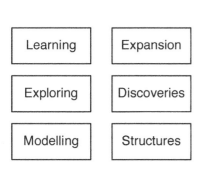

1 The Map of Experience – Burgess

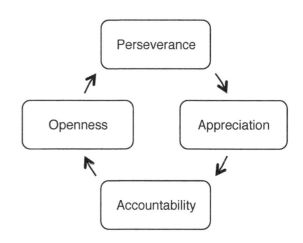

2 Collaborative Learning Model – The Northern School of NLP

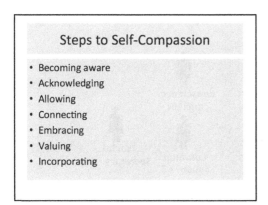

3 7 Steps to Self-Compassion – Bill O'Hanlon

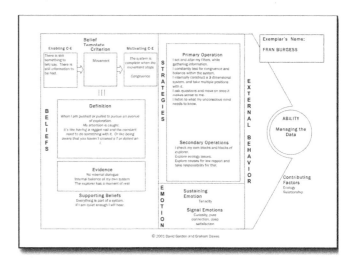

4 Managing Data – Burgess using Gordon/Dawes Experiential array

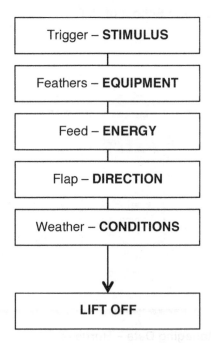

5   **Neurological Levels – Dilts**

My belief is that everyone has four drives that arise from deep within. These drives help the person decide their direction in life. While often these drives are used to help determine one's career path or life goals, I am using them here to decipher what plays out in marriage.

The four urges are: **blessed**, **blissed**, **pissed**, and **dissed**.

I'll detail each briefly.

Blessed involves the outpouring of goodness and talent you may be gifted with. When it comes to relationships, one of the members will be better at the romantic side of things, remembering important dates and events, taking care of the details for the family, or taking primary care of the kids. Blessed also could be the model your parent's relationship was for yours. The encouragement you receive from a mentor. The love you feel for your spouse because of their support and encouragement of you.

Blissed is the excited, joyful response you get when you think about the time you get to spend in your marriage. It is the response you feel when listening to good music. Or maybe reading poetry. It's doing whatever stirs something deep within your soul. Whatever turns you on, but not simply turning you on in the moment, it really fulfils something at your core.

Pissed refers to the areas in which you've been wronged or hurt. The stuff that makes you angry, upset, or just downright mad. Due to your exposure to these wounds, hurts, or frustrations, you will be more apt to recognize the same areas in others. Particularly your spouse. This could help you become more sensitive to others and their suffering, thus allowing for a closer connection.

Dissed means dissatisfied or disrespected. The times when you've been overlooked, taken for granted, dumped on one to many times. This also refers to the idea of being tired of the status quo.

6   **4 Marriage Drives: The Lazy Man's Guide to Marriage –
COREY**

source Bill O'Hanlon

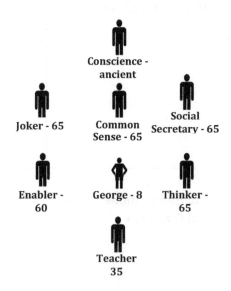

8   **A Parts Profile – Burgess**

7   **Preparing for Change – Burgess**

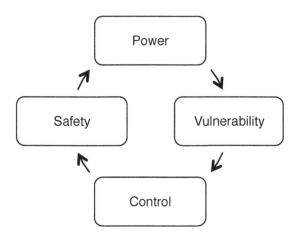

9   Model of Wellbeing – Burgess

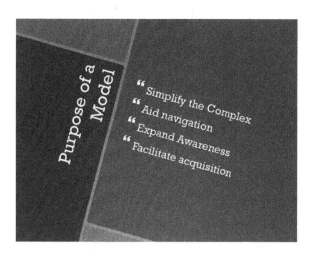

10   Purpose of a Model – Burgess

Labelling the Elements

Another contribution to the coherence of a model is down to the consistency of the language selected for the labels. Each element must be labelled in the same manner as each other. There cannot be a 'mixture of apples and oranges'. Therefore you need to know your 'grammar' and be able to distinguish between nouns, verbs and adjectives. You also need to have the ability to transform these labels into an equivalent archetype.

To develop your flexibility with proper labelling, come up with as many examples of Elements which can be labelled as Nominalisations, Verbs, Adjectives, Parts.

| | Nominalisation | Verb | | Adjective | Part/Archetype |
		Present	'ing' verb		
1.	Appreciation	Appreciate	Appreciating	Appreciative	The Fan
2.	Tenacity	Be Tenacious	Being Tenacious	Tenacious	The Stalwart
3.					
4.					
5.					
6.					
7.					
8.					
9.					
10.					

Delivery Methods

A model can be acquired in so many different ways – it is down to the designer to decide how this will be done.

What delivery method might you choose?

You are given a worked example so you can see what I am asking you to do. Then I am offering you six mini scenarios and asking you to come up with three different delivery methods, starting with your preferred option, along with your reasoning. At this stage, do not consider the treatment you are going to go for. That comes in the section on Technique Design. I then provide my suggested answers at the end of the workbook.

Worked example

Jan Ardui's *Excellence* model, you are given four elements – Discipline, Freedom, Performance and Alignment. You can opt to work with all four, or you could select two to develop first. You have a 20 minute slot for your technique. The group is predominately Procedural, Internally Referenced, more Thinking than Choice.

I have selected to go for:

- 1st = Choice – **Relational Constructs:** I would select two elements and work with them either through Confusion Technique or Cartesian Coordinates. I would frame this as a series of questions and make it content free. This cognitive approach with step by step stages would appeal to the group. This would take the explorer about 10 minutes, so if you were training it would be 20 minutes working in pairs.

- 1st = Choice – **Questions**: I would take all four elements and place them on a grid as part of a paper exercise, and again I would provide a cognitive series of questions. This would be appropriate if this model encapsulates the previous learning. The fun will be in the treatment I select using the frames. This approach again appeals to cognition and can be an individual exercise with enough time to complete in say 12-15 minutes and time to discuss outcomes.

- 3rd Choice – **Spatial Anchors:** Establish the four elements on the floor and work kinaesthetically through the four, responding to a simple pattern of questions. Since they are predominately Internally Referenced working individually would suit and only take 20 minutes. This would be ideal if the purpose was to gain access to a higher level of awareness through activating the relational field. This could be useful if you also want to break their habitual cognitive mindset.

Note: the first two options have equal merit so tie for first place.

The Bumper Bundle Companion Exercises

1 Working with Bill O'Hanlon's Model

You've been given written notes on Bill O'Hanlon's Blissed, Blessed, Pissed, Dissed model in tabular form. You have 1.5 hours to include a demonstration. The group is creative and adventurous, Proximity, Feeling and Move Towards.

Provide your three approaches and your reasons for that choice.

1

2

3

2 Working with Prochaska's Change Model

You've been given Prochaska's sequential Change Model – Precontemplation, Contemplation, Preparation, Action, Maintenance, Transformation, with a description of each stage. You have a slot after lunch. The group is Collaborative, Proactive, and Move Away From.

Provide your three approaches and your reasons for that choice.

1

2

3

3   Working with a Group Generated Model

The group has identified that Trust is lacking in their team. They have come up with three components which they consider contributes directly to levels of Trust – Respect, Outcome, Self Focus.

Provide your three approaches and your reasons for that choice.

1

2

3

4   Working with a Client Generated Model

You are now at the last 10 minutes of the session. You have been exploring with your client her responses to conflict and in the process she realises that she has a distinct ambivalence about her abilities and desires to confront. There will be a follow on session, so you want her to leave in a strong resourceful state.

Provide your three approaches and your reasons for that choice.

1

2

3

5   Working with McWhirter's Performance Model

You have McWhirter's hierarchical Performance, Management, Direction and Supervision model, which you know is quite impactful and deserves quality time given to it. You want to do something different and memorable. And it might serve to round off a day's training, or help dislodge a client's stuck state.

Provide your three approaches and your reasons for that choice.

```
1



2



3
```

6   Working with a Client Generated Model

You have a coaching client you have been seeing for some time. Change is happening. He has now fully recognised the issues which are holding him back and is currently exploring how he might deal with life without his habitual behaviour patterns. You have strong rapport with him. You feel your sessions may have become stale and you want to break the trance.

Provide your three approaches and your reasons for that choice.

```
1



2



3
```

Neurological Frames

Knowing your tradecraft requires an integrated understanding of the technology of the neurological frames. With this comes intuition to be applied in neurological modelling as well as technique design and construction.

Quiz

1 Which is the odd one out?

   a Meta Model

   b Milton Model

   c Metaphor.

2 Which is the odd one out?

   a Submodalities

   b Milton Model

   c Metaphor.

3 Which is the odd one out?

   a Parts

   b Multiple Perspectives

   c Reframing.

4 Which is the odd one out?

   a Space

   b Outcome Setting

   c Time.

5 Which is incorrect?

   a Altering VAK configuration changes state

   b VAK configuration is a Constructed Model

   c VAK structure is reflected in accessing cues and predicates.

6 Which is the odd one out?

   a VAK profiles define state

   b VAK configuration is personal and unique

   c VAK is only expressed in internal experience.

7 Which is incorrect?

   a Submodalities are not a modelling tool

   b Submodality configuration of an event changes over time

   c Submodalities are used as a calibration measurement.

8 Which is the odd one out?

   a Attractive, pleasant, unhappy

   b Large, close, grey

   c Loud, hazy, moving.

9 Which is the odd one out?

   a Colour, bright, staccato

   b Frightening, sore, ineffective

   c Heavy, moist, screeching.

10 Which is the odd one out?

   a Hungry, thirsty, empty

   b Green, hot, light

   c All around, moving, sour.

11 Which is the odd one out?

   a Fluffy, crispy, tasty

   b Dull, close, behind

   c Slow, shiny, rough.

12 Which is incorrect?

   a Time can be represented in Submodalities

   b Time can be represented in Mentors

   c Time can be represented in language.

13   Which is the incorrect?

   a Everyone has a Past, Present, Future

   b There is no one way to configure Time

   c Time construction is indicated through physiology.

14   Which is correct?

   a Our memories are stored at random irrespective of Time

   b It is advisable to approach the Past through a Dissociated position

   c Timelines are fixed.

15   Which is incorrect?

   a Temporal predicates are directly connected to Time

   b Spatial predicates are directly connected to Parts

   c Spatial predicates assist Association and Dissociation.

16   Which is correct? 2nd Position involves:

   a mind reading

   b stepping in and experiencing from our own perspective

   c stepping in and experiencing through the system of the other.

17   Which is correct? 3rd Position:

   a is a meta position looking at Self

   b involves a third party

   c views the relationship between 1st and 2nd position.

18   Which is correct? 4th Position is:

   a a dissociated 3rd Position

   b the relational field created within 1st, 2nd and 3rd

   c is meta to 1st Position.

19   Which is incorrect?

   a Dissociation occurs when on your timeline

   b Shifting the location of one element in a system will affect the other elements

   c Association and Dissociation are Submodality descriptions.

20   Which is incorrect?

   a Metaphor is a useful means of describing deep structure

   b Metaphor is used differently to Simile in NLP

   c Pacing Metaphor deepens rapport.

21   Which is correct?

   a Parts are standalone entities

   b Parts are literal descriptions of internal workings

   c Parts are expressions within an overall holistic system.

22   Which is incorrect?

   a Parts operate independently of each other

   b Parts are similar to Archetypes

   c Parts can be reconfigured.

23   Which is incorrect?

   a Mentors are a form of second positioning

   b Mentors have to be people we know

   c Mentors can provide profound insights.

24   Which is incorrect?

   a We cannot not Anchor

   b State is lessened through Anchoring

   c Adding Anchors to each other is called Stacking.

The Bumper Bundle Companion Exercises

Do You Know Your Techniques?

What neurological frames feature in each of these techniques?

	VAK	Submodalities	Time	Multiple Perspective	Space Associated/Dissociated	Metaphor	Mentors	Parts/Archetypes	Anchoring
6 Step Reframe									
Change Personal History									
Circle of Excellence									
Disney Strategy									
Meta Mirror									
Neurological Level Alignment									
New Behaviour Generator									
Phobia 'Cure'									
SCORE									
Swish									
Timeline Alignment									
Visual Squash									

What might you get...?

Here are a series of questions to test your understanding of Neurological Frames. You'll find suggested answers at the back.

1.   ... if you introduced Submodalities to an emotion/state?

2.   ... if you remove Mentors from Neurological Level Alignment?

3.   ... if you introduced Time into Meta Mirror?

4.   ... if you remove the initial VAK in the Phobia 'Cure'?

5.   ... if you remove the VAK in Circle of Excellence?

6.   ... if you based Neurological Level Alignment on one Part?

7.   ... if you introduced 2nd and 3rd Position in Timeline Alignment?

8.   … if you introduced Identity and Spirituality into Visual Squash?

9.   … if you introduced metaphor into SCORE?

10. …if you introduced Mentors into SCORE?

11. … if you introduced 2nd Position of The Dream, The Plan and The Criticism?

12. … if you introduced Past, Present and Future within a 6 Step Reframe?

13. … if you removed 2nd Position in Meta Mirror?

14. … if you applied Neurological Levels to a Belief?

15. … if you introduced Meta Model to a Belief?

Linguistic Frames

Having fluency in ALL the linguistic frames available to you should be your goal, if you set your sights on becoming an expert practitioner. If you are a natural linguist, then this should present little difficulty. If however you need to take the long route between conscious incompetence to conscious competence, then you need to practice, practice, review and practice some more. The results you achieve will be motivation enough.

What Are The Consequences?

Sometimes the Guide strays from the script within the instructions either through carelessness or a belief that he or she knows better. You have to be certain that your phrasing will produce the same outcomes. Identify where 'your' statement takes the explorer's attention. Does this match the intentions of the originator of the technique?

	The instruction reads:
	
	    Take moment now to notice
	
	And you say:
	
	    Take a moment now to see
		You would have taken your explorer into the visual rep system which may not be matching her internal system. If however this was because you had been tracking her eye movements and saw her accessing visually, then you have earned extra brownie points.

1	The instruction reads:
	
	    What new thoughts are you having?
	
	And you say:
	
	    What new thoughts did you have?	

2	The instruction reads:
	
	    Now complete these statements – I will know I have achieved…
	
	And you say:
	
	    Now complete these statements – You know you have achieved…	

3	The instruction reads:
	
	    What does this mean?
	
	And you say:
	
	    What's the significance of this?	

4	The instruction reads: How successful do you feel you can be? And you say: How successful do you know you are?	
5	The instruction reads: When you're ready, step out and move to … And you say: Move now to X.	
6	The instruction reads: Think of something you know you want to be. And you say: Think of something you know you want.	
7	The instruction reads: What are you now aware of? And you say: What's happening?	
8	The instruction reads: What stops you? And you say: What limitations are you becoming aware of?	
9	The instruction reads: What has happened to that sensation? Where has it gone? And you say: How are you feeling now?	

10	The instruction reads:	
	Knowing what you now know, continue your exploration until you come to a halt.	
	And you say:	
	When you're ready step off your line.	
11	The instruction reads:	
	How are you able to do that?	
	And you say:	
	What are you doing?	
12	The instruction reads:	
	Looking onto the situation, what have you realised as this mentor?	
	And you say:	
	Looking at the situation, what are you noticing?	
13	The instruction reads:	
	As this mentor, what do you want to say?	
	And you say:	
	What is the mentor saying?	
14	The instruction reads:	
	How does this resource connect with who you want to be?	
	And you say:	
	What's the connection between this state and the future You?	

What Do You Think?

Here are some questions to ponder on.

1	What makes trance language essential in Neurological Level Alignment?	
2	Where will you be using VAK predicates in Phobia 'Cure'?	
3	What particular language patterns do you need to pay attention to in Meta Mirror?	
4	What particular language patterns are essential for Timeline Alignment?	
5	Write out three reframes which are included specifically in the basic techniques	
6	If you are working with Beliefs, what language patterns would you be using?	
7	If you were to introduce submodalities and time, what language patterns would you be using?	
8	If you were working with Identity, what language patterns would you be using?	

Do You Know Your Techniques?

What Linguistic Frames are involved in each of these Techniques?

	Meta Model	Milton Model	Outcome Frame	Reframing	VAK Predicates	Temporal Predicates	Spatial Predicates Associative/Dissociative
6 Step Reframe							
Change Personal History							
Circle of Excellence							
Disney Strategy							
Meta Mirror							
Neurological Level Alignment							
New Behaviour Generator							
Phobia 'Cure'							
SCORE							
Swish							
Timeline Alignment							
Visual Squash							

Technique Deconstruction

If you aspire to knowing your craft inside out, then knowing how to deconstruct a technique to understand exactly how the effect was achieved is essential. This is profoundly true for anyone teaching NLP, especially when working with those becoming NLP trainers themselves.

Here, you are offered a worked example of Technique Deconstruction and then you are given three known techniques and two which will be unknown to you, to deconstruct for yourself. As ever suggested answers are at the back. I have also offered you my deconstructions of the other standard techniques found within the basic syllabus, to add to your resources. You may want to do some of them yourself before checking out what I have to say!

I have also included a couple of blanks for you to deconstruct some techniques of your choice.

I strongly suggest you revisit all the other techniques you know and test your understanding through deconstructing these as well. You'll gather that I consider this ability, based on integrated knowledge and understanding, to be too important to short change yourself!

Worked Example – Disney Strategy

Source: Robert Dilts

1   Standing in a neutral space, become aware of what you want to achieve. If you don't have something pre-defined, set yourself the intention of being open to what comes.   Allocate three spaces on the floor, as per the layout diagram.

2   **Dreamer**: Adopt the Dreamer physiology,

- Slow dream-like voice – I wish... What if... Just imagine if...
- Visual – eyes looking up and 'head in the clouds'
- Deep breathing
- Attracted towards ideas for the future, often covering a long time, main focus of attention rests on how it feels and looks.

Allow the Dreamer free rein to dream, to come up with as full a picture as possible of a vision or visions, with sounds and sensations. Resist any editing. Once you have some form of clarity, move on.

3   **Realist**: Adopt the Realist physiology.

- Practical, measured tones, reciting details – How can I... We have enough time to...
- Symmetrical movements, counting actions on fingers, feet on the ground, weighing up options
- Auditory eye movements, operates in the here and now
- Action orientated, looking at how ideas can be practically implemented, given the existing constraints and realities.

Let the Realist receive the dream, and draw up a plan of action to deliver it as it is presented, without any criticism. Once you have some form of clarity, move on. Place the Plan *in front* of the Realist.

4   **Critic**: Adopt the Critic physiology.

- tight often sharp tone, quick delivery – That won't work ... What happens when...
- often narrowed eyes and 'pursed lips', asymmetrical stance, often pointed finger and closed arms
- auditory digital
- full of logic, instinctively looking for the 'whys and why nots' to a given situation
- Questions are drawn from experience of past situations and projections of future ones, not satisfied until others have given good reasons.

Ask the Critic to identify those areas within *The Plan* which need further development.

Note: the Critic is not criticising the Realist, not the Realist's work.   Attention is on the dissociated Plan.

Package these concerns into a series of questions to give back to the Dreamer for answers. Ask your questions, using trancelike Dreamer voice, with softeners, like 'I'm wondering …' 'I'm curious …' etc. Guard against using a critical tone of voice.

5   Repeat 2 – 4, making adjustments, until all states are happy and at rest.

My Deconstruction

Technique Name : Disney Strategy	

Purpose: To turn dreams into reality	**Time:**15-20 mins

Calibrated Evidence: The Critic has no more to say.

Model Type	Methodology	Neurological	Linguistic
Constructed: Sequential	Kinaesthetic: using spatial anchors	Parts Perspectives Chaining Anchors	Milton Model Spatial Predicates

Skill Emphasis:

Maintaining spatial anchors

Calibrating maintenance of physiology for each of the Parts/Archetypes

Using trance intonation

Floor Layout – if relevant

Areas of Concern and Contingencies:

You need to make sure that it is the PLAN that is criticised and not The Realist or The Dreamer.

The Critic needs to form the objection in a question and delivered in a dreamlike way to establish rapport with the Dreamer.

The appropriate physiology for each of the Parts has to be established and maintained.

Comments:

Familiar Techniques

6 Step Reframe

Source: devised by Richard Bandler and John Grinder.

1   Identify the behaviour to be changed – a situation where you would like more choice. Check ecology.

2   Make contact with the Part responsible for the pattern, and ask if it wants to communicate with you. Establish a yes/no signal. If unsure, ask it to intensify that signal.

3   Thank the Part and find out the intent of the behaviour. And thank it for letting you know.

4   Request your Creative Part (or the Part that comes up with ideas) to find three new ways to satisfy the positive intention which do not have any undesirable consequences.

5   Ask the Part causing the unwanted behaviour to agree to one, some, or all of the three new ways before letting go of the old unwanted behaviour.   Thank it once it has agreed.   If it rejects any of the suggestions, go back to 4 and come up with some more if needs be.

6   Ecology check.

•   Will the new ways fit in with your life?

If the answer is 'No', ask:

•   What has to happen for you to feel OK about this change?

Enter into a negotiation process until the objecting Part is satisfied. You may have to go back to Step 2 and work with this Part to gain final resolution.

Your Deconstruction

Technique Name			
Purpose		Time	
Calibrated Evidence			
Model Type	Methodology	Neurological	Linguistic
Skill Emphasis		Floor Layout – if relevant	
Areas of Concern and Contingencies			
Comments			

Change Personal History

Source: devised by Richard Bandler and John Grinder.

1   Ask the explorer to identify an unwanted feeling or response that crops up and hinders a desired activity. As the guide, set **Kinaesthetic Anchor 1** to the unwanted or unpleasant feeling.

2   Apply Anchor 1 to assist the Explorer in going back through time to the earliest remembered instance, finding other times when he or she felt this way. Use phrases like:

   • Take this feeling and ride this feeling back into the past.

   • Let this feeling take you back to where it *really* belongs.

3   Keep applying Anchor 1. When you detect exaggerations of the expression, as the explorer is going back in time, stop him or her, and have them see the full experience, noting their age when the experience took place. Get the explorer to give each experience a name, so that you can both refer to them later on.

4   When the explorer has arrived at that first time, bring him or her back to the present and open their eyes. Now take off Anchor 1.

5   Looking onto the earliest experience, remind the explorer that 'This was a response because the Younger You didn't have any other resources. Since then you have developed so many more skills and gained so much more knowledge, which has given you a wide range of resources that the Younger You didn't have back then.'

   Now ask:

   • Which resource was needed at that time?

   • Access a time when you had that resource in just the way you want it now.

   Once the needed resource is identified, **establish Anchor 2** in a location different to that of the negative Anchor 1. (Make sure you can reach both locations comfortably at the same time.)

6   Have the Explorer go to the first identified experience. Here you collapse anchors by saying:

   • As you remember this negative state ... now take these resources to where they are really needed.

7   Fire the negative Anchor 1, and then the positive Anchor 2, and hold them both. Give the positive anchor a bit more pressure.

8   Go through each of the subsequent experiences, keeping these anchors on until the explorer comes back into the room with eyes open.

   Take the negative Anchor 1 off before you release the positive Anchor 2.

9   Test – Fire the negative Anchor 1 and see what happens. If you get a mild or indifferent response, then you have completed. If not, then you may have to go back and find an additional resource and recycle.

Your Deconstruction

Technique Name	

Purpose	Time

Calibrated Evidence

Model Type	Methodology	Neurological	Linguistic

Skill Emphasis	Floor Layout – if relevant

Areas of Concern and Contingencies

Comments

Neurological Level Alignment

Source: Robert Dilts.

1. Identify a situation in the near future, in which you want to be excellent.   In this situation, what is your Role? **You are an Excellent ...**

2. **Environment:** Move to the Environment space. As an Excellent ... in this environment, describe clearly what you see, what the sounds are, what it feels like externally and internally

3. **Behaviour:** Once you have identified the significant features of the Environment, move backwards to the Behaviour space.

    * Facing the Environment position, as an Excellent ... what specific things you are doing or saying?

    * Is there anything you would like to be doing better? Now think of someone who is particularly good at doing that. It can be anyone, real or fiction, alive or from the past. If he or she was here, where would they be standing or sitting?

    * Move to that spot. Ask this mentor – What advice would you like to give (your name), coming from your own excellence?

    * Return to your Behaviour spot and hear the advice being given to you. Acknowledge the presence of your mentor, knowing that he or she is there to be called upon at any time.

4. **Capability**: When you are ready, move backwards to your Capability space.

    * As an Excellent ... what are the specific skills and abilities you are using which enable you to do what you do?

    * Are there any more skills you would like to have? Now identify a mentor as before, and go through the same stages as in 3.

5. **Beliefs**: When you are ready, move backwards to your Belief space.

    * As an Excellent ... what values are important to? What do you believe to be true?

    * Are there any beliefs that you don't currently have which you know would serve you well? Is there anyone you know who holds these beliefs strongly? Now identify a mentor as before, and go through the same stages as in 3.

6. **Identity**: When you are ready, move backwards now to your Identity space.

    * As an Excellent ...   Who are you? What kind of Excellent ... are you? What metaphor or image best sums this up?

    * Is there a voice that supports this Identity?   Step into the source of the voice and go through the same stages as in 3.

7. **Spirituality**: Now move to your Spiritual space. Who else are you serving as you are an Excellent ...? What are you now aware of?

    Describe what you sense, in terms of what you are seeing. Turn round and step further into this space. Be aware of all the space around you, what you are hearing – perhaps it is complete silence, and allow your body, your arms to describe the space your experience takes up. Become aware of this moment, so that you can remember it and call it to mind any time you like. Anchor this state.

8. Taking your Spirituality experience, step back into the Identity space, experiencing both at the same time. Notice the differences, without describing them.

9. Take your experience of both your Spirituality and your Identity, and bring them into your Belief space. Notice the differences, without describing them.

10. Bring your Spirituality, Identity, and Beliefs into your Capability space. Notice the differences, without describing them.

11. Bring your Spirituality, Identity, Beliefs, and Capabilities into your Behaviour space. Notice the differences, without describing them.

12. Bring all levels of yourselves into your Environment space, and experience how it is transformed and enriched. Notice how you are feeling, locate the places in your body that hold these feelings of excellence. Notice the differences in sounds that are in your head. Notice the differences in the colours, your clarity of vision, and your sense of space. Standing there, connect with the source back there in your Spritual space, connect with the wisdom and deep knowledge, knowing that you bring this with you wherever you are.

NOTE: If ths submodalities have not shifted in the environment, then you need to go back up the line again, particularly to any point of earlier incongruence.

Your Deconstruction

Technique Name			
Purpose			Time
Calibrated Evidence			
Model Type	Methodology	Neurological	Linguistic
Skill Emphasis		**Floor Layout – if relevant**	
Areas of Concern and Contingencies			
Comments			

Unfamiliar Techniques

Crossing The Threshold

Model devised by Joseph Campbell – Hero's Journey.   Technique devised by Fran Burgess.

This exercise allows you to explore The Unknown safely, develop strategies for managing yourself, and discover ways where you can explore unknown situations to maximum effect.

1   Identify a large challenge that is ahead of you. It may be something that you have been putting off. It will certainly be something that will take you into uncharted waters. Mark out a line on the floor. This is your dividing line between Knowing and Not Knowing regarding this challenge.   Notice how much space you give to your Not Knowing area. You can adjust this to make it feel easier to travel.

2   Walk up to the line and be aware of the strength of your Not Knowing signal. If it is very weak, it may be because the challenge is actually not a difficult one after all. Consider a different challenge and test your signal again. You want it good and strong!

3   From this position, identify a safe spot on the other side which is accessible and on which you can stand once you have crossed the Threshold.

4   Each learning task requires a blend of physical, emotional, mental and spiritual learning. Identify a Mentor for each element.

-    Physical Mentor who has the strength and stamina to support the journey
-    Emotional Mentor who has wide emotional flexibility to respond to any situation
-    Mental Mentor who is able to plan, problem solve and evaluate
-    Spiritual Mentor who understands guiding connection at a higher level

6   With each Mentor step into where they are and listen to the advice they have to offer you, returning each time to the central position. Once you have gathered all four, invite them to stand behind you, so that you can continue to be aware of their energy and support.

7   Stand back and identify any additional resources you need before crossing the line. Go to these places where you already have these resources, re-access them, and bring them to the line.

8   Now walk across the line to your safe spot. If you have any difficulty in crossing, check out if you need additional resources or consult your Mentors. Notice if there are any areas you want to avoid. Approach them, circle them, and gather any new information you need. You may find on closer inspection that the area is not as bad as you thought.

-    What do you need to pay attention to?
-    What resources do you need for this?

9   Cross back over your line, bringing with you all your new understanding.

-    Now step up to the edge of your map, the point between Knowing and Not Knowing.
-    Has it shifted? How are you now responding to being on the edge of Not Knowing?

Your Deconstruction

Technique Name			
Purpose		Time	
Calibrated Evidence			
Model Type	Methodology	Neurological	Linguistic
Skill Emphasis		Floor Layout – if relevant	
Areas of Concern and Contingencies			
Comments			

Box 9

Model devised by John McWhirter – From In To.   Technique devised by Fran Burgess

1   Step into each Box:

- Register your level of wellbeing.

- What does it feel like? What are you doing? What are you thinking?

- What does this tell you?

2   Step outside the space and look onto each of the Boxes.

- Which ones seem 'dangerous'? Which ones are 'safe'? Which ones are unimportant?

- Can you remember a similar situation in the past, which you have learnt from?

- How do the submodalities differ for each – size, shape, colour? How might you alter these?

- What resources do you need to tackle the 'dangerous' ones?

3   Gather these resources, and step back into the 'dangerous' ones.

- What do you now notice?

- What is now possible?

4   Think of a new situation coming up which would have been scary. Go through each of the Boxes, and make whatever adjustment you need to make so that you feel equal to whatever this new situation may bring.

Your Deconstruction

Technique Name	

Purpose	Time

Calibrated Evidence			

Model Type	Methodology	Neurological	Linguistic

Skill Emphasis	Floor Layout – if relevant

Areas of Concern and Contingencies

Comments

Your Deconstruction

Technique Name			
Purpose		Time	
Calibrated Evidence			

Model Type	Methodology	Neurological	Linguistic

Skill Emphasis	Floor Layout – if relevant

Areas of Concern and Contingencies

Comments

Your Deconstruction

Technique Name			
Purpose		**Time**	
Calibrated Evidence			
Model Type	**Methodology**	**Neurological**	**Linguistic**
Skill Emphasis		**Floor Layout – if relevant**	
Areas of Concern and Contingencies			
Comments			

Technique Construction

Case Study

This is the same Case Study provided in the Delivery Method section (page 101). There we were given the Model, and I came up with three possible Delivery Methods to choose from. Here you are to decide if the delivery method will be sufficient to carry the technique and bring the model alive, or if we need to add more technology to bring more life and direction into it.

You've been given Jan Ardui's *Excellence Model*, which has four elements – Discipline, Freedom, Performance and Alignment. You can opt to work with all four, or you could select two to develop first. You have a 20minute slot for your technique. The group is predominately Procedural, Internally Referenced, more Thinking than Choice.

Treatment 1

Relational Constructs: I would select two elements and work with them either through Confusion Technique or Cartesian Coordinates. I would frame this as a series of questions and make it content free. This cognitive approach with step by step stages would appeal to the group. This would take the explorer about 10 mins, so if you were training it would be 20 mins working in pairs.

I am opting to take two pairs and work them using Cartesian Coordinates and Beliefs to Identity from Neurological Levels.

Good Performance Poor Alignment	Good Performance Good Alignment
Poor Performance Poor Alignment	Poor Performance Good Alignment

This causes the explorer to draw on a reference experience to make sense of that combination of coordinates, and then focus specifically onto the beliefs, values and identity in that moment. I am choosing to go for present continuous tense to create a through time experience, the summing it up in a metaphorical identity, as a means of strengthening association.

An example of the process would be:

When I have poor alignment and poor performance:

- I am believing …

- I am valuing …

- I am like …

Why might this work?

What might be the drawbacks of this technique?

Treatment 2

Questions: I would take all four elements and place them on a grid as part of a paper exercise, and again I would provide a cognitive series of questions. This would be appropriate if this model encapsulates the previous learning. The fun will be in the treatment I select using the frames. This approach again appeals to cognition and can be an individual exercise with enough time to complete in say 12-15 mins and time to discuss outcomes.

This time I would select Meta Model to expand the system and explore and extend the underpinning beliefs the explorer holds regarding Excellence. This would be a lovely way to illustrate the Meta Model at work, especially if the explorers have already covered it – theoretically.

A. Performing Well	B. Having Freedom
C. Being Disciplined	D. Being Aligned

An example of the process would be covering each of the boxes with the following:

1   A, B, C, D means I can … I must …

2   A, B, C, D leads to … because … since …

3   People who are A, B, C, D deserve …

You'll notice that I have assumed that the explorer has good reference experiences of each of the elements. This presupposition forces her to come up with positive illustrations from her own map, and in turn will generate a meta cognition at a higher level of awareness.

Why might this work?

What might be the drawbacks of this technique?

Treatment 3

Spatial Anchors: Establish the four elements on the floor and work kinaesthetically through the four, responding to a simple pattern of questions. Since they are predominately Internally Referenced working individually would suit and only take 20 mins. This would be ideal if the purpose was to gain access to a higher level of awareness through activating the relational field. This could be useful if you also want to break their habitual cognitive mindset.

I would base this in a context where they have previously been excellent to their own satisfaction. Using the four spatial locations, I would invite them to step into each spot and identify the relevant level relative to their chosen context. I may then go for metaphor, or a somatic gesture, or possibly a comment. If they were dominantly externally referenced, I would probably add mentors inviting second positioning.

Performance	**Freedom**
Discipline	**Alignment**

Once all four spaces have been modelled out, I would then look at the relationships between the squares and their dynamics. Finally each explorer would step into the centre of the process and experience the impact of their heightened awareness as it affects this context. This would be future paced with an upcoming situation demanding personal excellence.

Why might this work?

What might be the drawbacks of this technique?

Your Turn

Scenario 1

Preframe

You've been given Prochaska's Change model which is sequential in six stages. You have the 1.5 hour slot after lunch. The group is Collaborative, Proactive, and Move Away From. Identify a technique that would involve Spatial Anchors. How might you incorporate association, dissociation and submodalities?

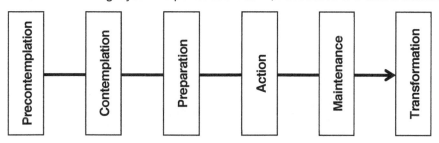

Prochaska's Change Model

Scenario 2

Preframe

The group has identified that Trust is lacking in their team. They have come up with a three element simultaneous model which they consider contributes directly to Trust.

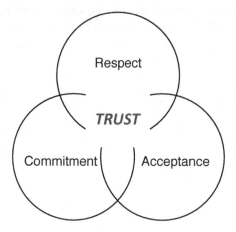

Select a technique with Spatial Anchors and incorporate second positioning.

Scenario 3

Preframe

You are now at the last 10 minutes of the session. You have been exploring with your client her responses to conflict and in the process she realises that she has a distinct ambivalence about her abilities and desires to confront. There will be a follow on session, so you want her to leave in a strong resourceful state.

Given the limited timeframe, you may want to explore the beliefs and resources within. Devise a process which uses Mentors and Acting As If.

Writing Instructions

Case Study Instructions

I have deliberately written the following instructions badly for the treatments offered in the previous section. When I say 'badly', they don't conform to all the criteria set down, and there may be some technological errors here. Your task is to evaluate the instructions for the following.

Technical Accuracy: Second position the explorer's experience. Is the process logical? Does it flow progressively? Is it capable of delivering the outcome?

Linguistic Accuracy: Does the language match the structure? Does it deliver the intended outcome? Does it target the explorer's attention precisely?

Constants	Content	Considerations
Title	Outcome	End User
Source Acknowledgement	Evidence	Layout
Date	Numbered Steps	Style
Model	Calibration	Meta Comments
Length	Future Pace	
Comments	Comments	Comments

Instructions for Treatment 1

Generating Excellence

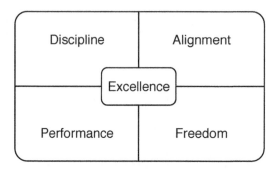

1   Answer the following questions. Your partner may write down your answers so that you have a copy for future reference.

 •   When I have poor alignment and poor performance, I believe ..., I value ..., I am like ...

 •   When I have poor alignment and good performance, I believe ..., I value ..., I am like ...

 •   When I have good alignment and poor performance, I believe ..., I value ..., I am like ...

 •   When I have good alignment and good performance, I believe ..., I value ..., I am like ...

 •   When I am excellent, I believe ..., I value ..., I am like ...

2   Now consider a task that you want to excel at. Have your partner read out your answers. What is happening? What's your evidence? What could you do differently?

The Bumper Bundle Companion Exercises

Appraisal of Instructions

Technical Accuracy: Second position the explorer's experience. Is the process logical? Does it flow progressively? Is it capable of delivering the outcome?

Linguistic Accuracy: Does the language match the structure? Does it deliver the intended outcome? Does it target the explorer's attention precisely?

Constants	Content	Considerations
Title	Outcome	End User
Source Acknowledgement	Evidence	Layout
Date	Numbered Steps	Style
Model	Calibration	Meta Comments
Length	Future Pace	
Comments	Comments	Comments

Instructions for Treatment 2

Generating Excellence

by Fran Burgess (2011) based on a model devised by Jan Ardui.

1   Ask your explorer:

• How comfortable are you with the thought of being excellent?   1 low-10 high

2   Have your explorer read out his/her answers and write them down.

Being aligned means	Good Performance means	Discipline means	Having freedom means
you can…			
you must…			
Being aligned leads to	Good Performance leads to	Discipline leads to	Having freedom leads to
because…			
since …			
People who are aligned deserve …	Good Performance deserves …	Disciplined people deserve …	People who have freedom deserve …

3   Ask your explorer:

• How comfortable are you *now* with the thought of being excellent?   1 low-10 high

4   Ask your explorer to consider a task or project that is coming up.

• What challenges are his/she now prepared to set?

The Bumper Bundle Companion Exercises

Appraisal of Instructions

Technical Accuracy: Second position the explorer's experience. Is the process logical? Does it flow progressively? Is it capable of delivering the outcome?

Linguistic Accuracy: Does the language match the structure? Does it deliver the intended outcome? Does it target the explorer's attention precisely?

Constants	Content	Considerations
Title	Outcome	End User
Source Acknowledgement	Evidence	Layout
Date	Numbered Steps	Style
Model	Calibration	Meta Comments
Length	Future Pace	
Comments	Comments	Comments

Instructions for Treatment 3

Generating Excellence

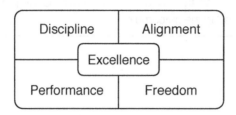

You may find that there are occasions when you want to display your excellence. There may be certain occasions which call for you to draw upon your excellence. You may find it difficult to consider your own excellence. You may feel that it is inappropriate to stand out from others. Alternatively you may be feeling frustrated knowing there is more to you that is not coming out. Whatever your response to excellence and your need for it, this process will enable you to become more comfortable with accessing your excellence and proving to yourself and others just how much you have to offer, naturally and instinctively. You would want that wouldn't you?

1   **Discipline**: What discipline do you exercise? What does this feel like? Where do you keep this feeling in your body? What gesture sums up your sense of discipline? What phrase comes to mind?

2   **Freedom**: What freedom do you display? What does this feel like? Where do you keep this feeling in your body? What gesture sums up your sense of discipline? What phrase comes to mind?

3   **Performance**: How well do you perform? What does this feel like? Where do you keep this feeling in your body? What gesture sums up your sense of discipline? What phrase comes to mind?

4   **Alignment**: How much alignment do you achieve? What does this feel like? Where do you keep this feeling in your body? What gesture sums up your sense of discipline? What phrase comes to mind?

5   Now step into each of the spaces once more. You can choose which one to go to first. From this place look at the other three. What is the relationship between this element and the other three? How are they connected? How do these influence your experience in this space? You may want to walk between them to see if there are any blockages. What are these blockages like? How might you unblock them?

6   When you are completely finished Step 5, step into the centre.

7   Anchor this.

- How high is your level of excellence?   1 low-10 high
- What does this feel like? Where do you keep this feeling in your body?
- What gesture sums up your sense of discipline? What phrase comes to mind?

The Bumper Bundle Companion Exercises

Appraisal of Instructions

Technical Accuracy: Second position the explorer's experience. Is the process logical? Does it flow progressively? Is it capable of delivering the outcome?

Linguistic Accuracy: Does the language match the structure? Does it deliver the intended outcome? Does it target the explorer's attention precisely?

Constants	Content	Considerations
Title	Outcome	End User
Source Acknowledge-ment	Evidence	Layout
Date	Numbered Steps	Style
Model	Calibration	Meta Comments
Length	Future Pace	
Comments	Comments	Comments

Your Own Instructions

Taking each of these exercises, write up your own instructions for them, in line with the criteria.

You also have instructions to complete for the three techniques proposed in the Technique Constuction section, the one based on the Prochaska Model, one on a Trust Model and one based on Conflict.

You will find finished suggestions for each of these techniques at the end of the workbook.

And Finally

You have now come to the end of this series of exercises. I hope you have found them challenging, stimulating and rewarding. I also hope in the process that you have been rewarded for your knowledge.

I am assuming that you've been checking your progress against the suggested answers I've provided in the section that follows. Obviously there are likely to be differences between the answers I've provided and your own, since much is a matter of opinion. That said, I hope my answers offer you a useful perspective and add to your own knowledge and learning.

Most importantly, however, I hope you are inspired to go out there and practice your new found knowledge wherever you can. The more skillful you become, through trial, error and feedback, the more elegant your performance will be – all to the benefit of your clients, explorers and end users.

You are part of a fantastic lineage. Enjoy flexing your mind and modelling muscles. Let the words trip from your tongue. And let the spirit of NLP soar through you from your heart!

The Bumper Bundle Companion Exercises

Suggested Answers

Suggested Answers

Attitude

The Personality of a Modeller

Modelling Occupations

Anthropologists, Archaeologists, Architects, Business Consultants, Car Mechanics, Choreographers, Coaches, Dancers, Detectives, Doctors, Engineers, Explorers, Film Directors, Gossip Columnists, Judges, Mothers, Musicians, Painters, Pathologists, Research Scientists, Sculptors, Therapists, Trackers

Underpinning Philosophy

Quiz

1b, 2a, 3c, 4a, 5a, 6b, 7a, 8b, 9c, 10a, 11b, 12a, 13a, 14b, 15b, 16a

Methodology

The Modelling Process

The Modelling Route Map

Quiz

1a, 2c, 3b, 4c, 5b, 6c, 7c, 8a, 9a, 10b

Plot The Route

Application Area	End User	Focus of Enquiry	Source(s) of Information	Types of Intervention	Types of Outcome
Personal Development	Self	Desired	Literature	Neurological Modelling	Exploration/identification of Structure
Consultant	Host Organisation	Unwanted	Exemplars	Intuitive Modelling Methodology	Exploration/identification of Structure
Therapist	Exemplar	Unwanted	Exemplar	Neurological Modelling	Restructuring
Therapist /Trainer	Third party	Desired	Self, Exemplars	Neurological and Linguistic Modelling	Model Construction Model Acquisition
Coach	Exemplar	Unwanted	Exemplar	Process model	Restructuring

Modelling Interventions

Quiz

1a, 2b, 3c, 4c, 5c, 6a, 7c, 8c, 9a, 10a

Neurological Modelling

Submodalities, multiple perspectives, time, mentors, metaphors, parts/archetypes

Linguistic Modelling

Meta model, milton model, outcome frame, reframing (sleight of mouth) clean language, sensory, temporal and spatial predicates, neurological levels, metaprogramme questions

Modelling Methodologies

Quiz

1c, 2c, 3a, 4b, 5b, 6b, 7a, 8c, 9b, 10c

Suggested Answers

Which Would You Choose?

	Methodology	Comment
1.	Unconscious Uptake	You will be able to pick up how she does what she does by paying attention to her physiology and where her attention goes.
2.	Experiential Array	You could develop the array for the unwanted oontext and also for the one which is free of the trait. Your exemplar can then compare both, and take on the useful one.
3.	Analytical Modelling	Working with the SCORE model, your participants can agree the current problems, gain consensus on outcome and identify with and connect to the desired effects of this before acknowledging the causes without dwelling on them. At this stage resources can be quickly identified and evaluated. This information, plus the meta comments expressed along the way, may be sufficient to draw up a range of models.
4.	Symbolic Modelling	This client will find it easy to access the symbolic metaphors required for this approach. She will have no need for cognitive language and let the metaphors speak for her. And this approach is predominately future outcome focussed which will take her to whre she wants to get to.
5.	Somatic Modelling	The free expression within this approach would appeal, especially if activities have been more cognitively orientated. Somatics lend themselves to expressing shifts in physiology through time.
6.	Punctuation Modelling	This approach is quick and effective, so everyone can have their own model, in this instance regarding how they approach learning, within 10 – 15 minutes. In the process they will have gained a first hand experience of the nature of structure and how it relates directly to behaviour and state.

Relationship Skills

Pitfalls and Antidotes

Scenario 1

This exemplar irritates you. She is a highly privieged young woman who has been given so much. She seems really arrogant, unware of her good fortune and dismissive of others. She finds it hard to answer you questions, often coming to a halt with 'Don't know', making out that it is down to your poor questioning.

Guard against

- 'Boxing her ears' !
- Projecting your judgement onto her through meta comment or loaded questions.
- Losing your sense of connection and your modelling state.
- Providing answers for her.
- Giving up.

Antidotes

- Reconnect through centering and widening your field/bubble once more to include her.
- Remind yourself of your outcome.
- Deepen rapport through providing universals to acknowledge how difficult it can be to find answers to your unusual questions. Remind her that there are no 'right' answers, only the ones she comes up with.
- Look behind the 'Can't'. Check out what might be limiting her and what she feels the consequences of her answers might be.
- Consider adopting a different methodology.

Scenario 2

You are seeking to model out the unwanted behaviour. Through meta model questioning you are seeking to access the limiting beliefs which are driving your exemplar's behaviour. Your exemplar is looking increasingly uncomfortable, and the flow of his responses is slowing up, which you put down to the unfamiliarity of the territory you are exploring, so you press on.

Guard against

- Pursuing your own outcomes to the detriment of rapport and client resourcefulness.
- Deciding for yourself the causes of the discomfort without checking it out.
- Believing that you know better than your exemplar regarding what your exemplar needs.

Antidotes

- Take a meta position and describe your experience eg: Fran is asking questions and David is finding it hard to answer them. 'What needs to happen?'
- Widen the system and consider other pressures which may be on the exemplar – the time is overrunning and he has to get home by a certain time, or he might be needing to go to the loo, or you have inadvertently upset him, or he is uncertain what you are going to do with this information.
- Have a look at your levels of rapport – your energy, his energy.
- Check what he believes about beliefs. Check what he thinks might happen if he finds out what is behind his behaviour.
- Invite him to step into 3rd position and ask him what he thinks David and Fran need to do.

Scenario 3

Exemplar has agreed to be part of your list of exemplars, and felt gratified that you had asked. However she leads an erratic life, with shared child care arrangements with ex, a partner who works shifts, and she is a supply teacher. She had cancelled several appointments and so you arranged an evening meeting, which she also cancelled at the last minute. She has arrived late for the rearranged, rearranged session. You are up against a deadline yourself.

Guard against

- Entering into her chaos and turning your own routines upside down in the name of flexibility.
- Sharing responsibility for her chaos.
- Feeling bad about taking up her time.
- Offering coaching services!

Antidotes

- By way of review, go through the formal contracting process once more, or possibly for the first time.
- Suggest that she has taken on too much, and it would be fine if she withdrew.
- See if you can link her management of her chaos with the desired behaviour that you are wanting to model.

Scenario 4

Your exemplar is your son's girlfriend, and she has been put forward for coaching by the organisation. She is highly ambitious and he is not, and they are currently going through a bad patch. You've had stories from your son who is really upset, but have not spoken to her. She seems reluctant to speak freely with you.

Guard against

- Blurring roles.
- Becoming emotionally involved.
- Operating out of your own map.
- Stopping from including your son in the discussions, or in any way justifying his actions.

Antidotes

- Declare your conflict of interests with the employer and refer to another Coach.
- Only continue if you are clear that you want to help her achieve her outcomes, even if it may adversely affect your son.
- Contract clearly regarding the scope of the Coaching relationship.
- Establish her coaching outcome and monitor that *all* of your interventions are directly serving it.

Scenario 5

Your exemplar is describing a family issue, involving her husband's family – in particular her brother-in-law – and how badly it is affecting her and her husband. She is estranged from her own family and relies heavily on all being well here. She feels the loss of her connection with her brother-in-law. Since nothing particularly serious seems to have happened, especially not to her, you are wondering what all the fuss is about.

Guard against

- Dismissing or discounting the severity of the problem.
- Offering reframes or platitudes.
- Deciding quickly who is at fault.
- Taking too narrow a view on what is happening.

Antidotes

- Test the nature of the relationship with brother-in-law.
- Test the nature of the marriage.
- Look beyond the immediate relationships. Plot the full family system to discover the relationships held within it. Identify the roles each one takes up, in particular the brother-in-law.

Scenario 6

Your exemplar has come to you to be rid of a flying phobia. You have allocated one hour, and after a short introduction, you intend to take him through the standard Fast Phobia 'Cure'. By way of subsequent chat, he mentions issues about being an anxious car passenger and having problems at work, which you don't have time to go into.

Guard against

- Automatically believing the client, so skimp on the preliminaries.
- Promising a quick solution.
- Putting too much reliance on a technique and trusting the technique more than the client.
- Feeling bad that the process might take longer and cost more than you had suggested.

Antidotes

- Take a full history, even though the issue seems self explanatory.
- Resist the temptation to automatically kick into the 'obvious' technique.
- Operate from the wider system and notice patterns – in this case the need for control.

Scenario 7

You have identified three exemplars who have agreed to be interviewed or modelled by you. If took some time to identify and pin them down. You are aware of the time commitment they are offering. One of them is your line manager and you are anxious to acquit yourself well. Another is a friend, and another is someone you've been introduced to.

You find that an element from your boss's information jars with your values. And the third exemplar has to cancel at short notice.

Guard against

- Jettisoning the whole project.
- Rejecting your boss's data out of hand – or of making a judgement against your boss.
- Being pressurised into finding a replacement third exemplar.
- Feeling resentful and stressed by the process.
- Losing your curiosity.

Antidotes

- Keep the End User in mind. They won't know the sources of your model. They are only interested in acquiring a model which serves their purposes.
- Can you process your boss's data through your own value system. Does it still work? What amendments might you have to make?
- If you have the time, get another situation where the boss applies this skill and notice any useful differences here.
- Find a third exemplar if readily accessible.
- Drop your first and third exemplar; go with your friend, ensuring that you sample at least three situations of the skills you value.

Scenario 8

You have been given the fantastic opportunity to model a personal hero. You have decided to go for a particular approach since it is one that you are comfortable with and feel confident about using. You have your recording equipment at the ready. However your exemplar doesn't seem to want to follow your line of questioning. He seems to believe he knows what you need to know and goes about telling you. He definitely avoids answering questions that take him to unfamiliar places.

Guard against

- Being in awe of your hero and becoming submissive.
- Getting frustrated that he is not following your lead.
- Despairing that you are about to waste this great opportunity.

Antidotes

- Stand back and evaluate which bits of information you are getting which fit with what you are looking for. You don't have to go through the process as it is written in the book.
- Back track and confirm what you have got. Ask: 'If this was all I knew would I be able to do your X?' Notice the holes and gaps.
- Use your back tracking to set up an altered state and slip in the questions that might provoke resistance.
- Mentally tear up your modelling methodology and go for another format.
- Be prepared to stop and put your flag somewhere else. It might be that he is wanting that as well.

Scenario 9

During your session with your exemplar, you noted that she waves her hands about a lot and uses lots of expressive facial gestures. She has particularly striking manicured nails and several expensive looking rings. Again she is carefully madeup and dominantly applied lipstick. To avoid being distracted by this effusive show, you focus on what she is saying and the patterns that are emerging, in line with her outcome

Guard against

- Deleting her non verbal gestures.
- Forming a value judgement about her appearance.
- Failing to spot patterns between the behaviours and content.

Antidotes

- Register your judgements, relax and soften your focus.
- Shift your focus of attention.
- Calibrate any patterns emerging from the hand movements and facial gestures.
- Become curious about what is located at the spaces marked out by the hand movements, or eye movements.

Scenario 10

This is your fourth exemplar. You have a pretty good idea of what the emerging model might be and you sense you are going through the motions here. In fact you realise that this exemplar deviates from the others and isn't really contributing anything of value.

Guard against

- Making early assumptions.
- Shoehorning the data you are getting into a model that is in danger of becoming prematurely fixed.
- Ceasing to be curious.

Antidotes

- Remind yourself about what this exemplar does particularly well, and your reasons for selecting him
- Be curious about the differences. Refer back to your notes to see if you had overlooked anything similar.
- Find out why these differences are important to this individual.
- Consider using this content for possibly a different enquiry under a different class of behaviour.

Scenario 11

You are thoroughly enjoying your session with this exemplar. You've hit it off well and he seems really into the process and is a pleasure to work with. His answers are seemingly honest and disarming, and he is fascinated by what your questions are bringing forth. He is entertaining and provides some fabulous anecdotes to illustrate what he is saying.

Guard against

- Being seduced by his charisma and flattered by his responsiveness.
- Sharing maps so closely that you are not noticing differences.
- Confusing the role of modeller with blossoming friend.
- Squandering time.
- Allowing him to 'get carried away' and enter into entertaining mode and not maintain serious enquiry.

Antidotes

- Use relevancy challenges.
- Remind him of the modelling outcome.
- Keep backtracking and clarify the hard content that you have gathered.
- Constantly step into the data and monitor if you are getting a reference experience that links to the desired behaviour.
- If appropriate suggest meeting up informally later on.

Scenario 12

You are now in the position to construct your own original technique from the model you have created. You have spent a lot of time wondering what you are going to do. You are presenting your workshop around your findings in a couple of days time, and have heard that it has been reduced to 3 hours.

Guard against

- Wanting to include the kitchen sink into the technology of your technique. Keep it simple.
- Taking up a disproportionate amount of time on this technique within the programme.
- Feeing resentful that the day's programme has been denied to you.

Antidotes

- Find a way of streamlining the process, either through a work sheet of questions, presenting from the front, or introducing a story or trance.
- Abandon the technique for this workshop in readiness for another later on.

Meta Messages

Exercise 1

Behaviour	Possible Intended Meta Message	Possible Received Meta Message
1 Turns up late for sessions.	I am important and terribly busy.	You are disorganized and disrespectful.
2 Favours one learner more than the others.	You are important to me.	You don't know how to manage a group.
3 Wears smart expensive clothing.	I am successful and a good investment.	Put your mouth where your wallet is.
4 Refers to own teachers and training events attended.	I honour my lineage of learning.	You are a name dropper.
5 Listens attentively to questions.	I want to understand.	Everyone is important to you.
6 Reads a novel whilst group is undertaking a set task.	You can manage on your own.	How disrespectful.
7 Congruently admits to not knowing something.	It's OK not to know something.	It's OK not to know something.
8 Tells self deprecating stories about own learning experiences.	Learning has its setbacks for everyone.	Learning has its setbacks for everyone.

Establishing and Re-establishing Relationship

Question 1

This is your exemplar's first session with you. He has issues with control. He has recently been seeing a CBT counsellor referred to by his GP. Already he has contradicted several things you have said.

Pace:

1   I'm impressed your commitment to yourself and your wellbeing which means you are prepared to give therapy another chance.

2   I know that initially NLP may seem a strange approach, certainly being different to CBT in key ways.

3   And it is great that you won't let me get away with anything that doesn't fit with you.

Lead: Yet sometimes even greater control can be gained after letting go of misplaced certainty now.

Suggested Answers

Question 2

> Your exemplar finds it really hard to talk about a certain subject and is constantly avoiding all reference to it.
>
> 1   It is never easy to find the words to describe something that has been hidden for a long time.
>
> 2   And you may be fearing what might come up when you do.
>
> 3   Or you may be fearing my response.
>
> Lead: And happily your unconscious mind will let you know when it is safe to go there, and I will be here for you as we welcome the new Information.

Question 3

> Your client the Training Manager has taken exception to something you have just said.
>
> 1   You are right, that was clumsy and thoughtless of me. I'm sorry. I wasn't paying sufficient attention to what I was saying.
>
> 2   I realise I was making a judgement from my own experience and not considering what was happening from your organisation's point of view.
>
> 3   You were right to correct me.
>
> Lead: I hope I haven't offended you. Where can we go from here?

Question 4

> Your Coaching exemplar is concerned that you will think she is stupid, and wrong to have the thoughts she has.
>
> 1   Being concerned about what others think is a natural response.
>
> 2   Sometimes, however ,such concerns get in the way of finding out what you actually believe yourself.
>
> 3   Everyone is different, and I have no way of knowing how I would respond in your situation.
>
> Lead: So bite the bullet, and say what you're thinking. You may surprise yourself!

Question 5

> Your Contracting Manager is raising questions about the effectiveness of the enquiry process to date.
>
> Pace:
>
> 1   I understand that you had hoped to have something to report by now. So did I.
>
> 2   I know that the reasons for the delays never look good after the event.
>
> 3   And you may be worried that the budget is running out of hand.
>
> Lead: So can we work out how we can use the information we have gathered so far, and plan how to accommodate the delay into the next stage of the project.

Question 6

> You have introduced an exercise requiring the participants to step into various spatial anchors arranged on the floor. You have met resistance in some quarters.
>
> Pace:
>
> 1   This process may feel strange to some of you, and you are wondering what world you've entered into!
>
> 2   The inquisitive amongst you can look forward to what you are about to discover.
>
> 3   And it is a great excuse to get out of your chairs and move about.
>
> Lead: However, if you really feel uncomfortable doing this, find yourself a flat surface to work on and let your fingers do the walking instead. You will get almost as good an experience as the others.

Suggested Answers

Question 7

You want to book an hour of a senior manager's time to be an exemplar, and she is showing some reluctance regarding its usefulness.

Pace:

1   I know you are busy, but you may like to do something totally different to learn more about how you are good at doing what you do.

2   As a manager, I assume you are always on the look out for different approaches you can take yourself with your staff.

3   And there are few who are as fascinating as ourselves!

Lead: So this is an opportunity for you to discover just what makes you good at what you do, and a way of being able to bring others up to your level of operation.

Question 8

You have spent time with key senior supervisors and are presenting your findings to the General Manager. He has become defensive and is unreceptive to hearing your evidence.

Pace:

1   It can't be easy hearing what your staff are thinking but haven't be able to tell you themselves.

2   You may also be thinking this is taken to being a reflection on your management abilities, which it is not.

3   And obviously we aren't focussing on all the elements that are working well. If they weren't, the problems would have had a much greater impact.

Lead: Instead of taking this personally, be grateful that you now know, so that you can do something about it before it really gets out of hand.

Working With Data

Thinking Logically

Exercise 1 – Logical Types

- What are its **dimensions**?
- What is its level of **complexity**?
- What is this **a part of**?
- What is this **an example of**?
- What is this **similar to**?
- What is **made of**?
- What does this **do**?
- What are the **benefits** of this?

- What is the **purpose** of this?
- What is the **need** for this?
- What does this **represent**?
- What does this **symbolise**?
- What does this **infer**?
- What are its **aesthetics**?
- What does it **cater** for?
- What is it **associated** with?
- What is **held within?**

- What is **on the outside**?
- What does it **become**?
- What has it **been previously**?
- What can it be **made into**?
- What **era** does it belong to?
- What **sources** does it draw on?

Exercise 2 – Widening Thinking

Part of a square
Part of a window
Part of organisational chart
A number
A letter of the alphabet
A line
A symbol
A arrow without a point
A baton

A string of liquorice
A series of dots
A package of pixels
A form of light energy
A direction indicator
A line on the road
A divider
A boundary/border
An aerial

A lightning conductor
A telegraph pole
A prop
A measuring tape
A rocket
A thin blue line
A line of blood
A crack in the door
An edge of a page

A stage flap from above
A thin man without a head
A torch beam
A vapour trail
A tyre track
A scorch mark of a meteor
A shooting star
A stalk with no leaves
A tossed caber

Exercise 3 – Widening Thinking More

A window pane
A hot cross bun
Part of a snowflake
A corner of patchwork
Spokes in a wheel
A laced shoe
A symbol
Multiplication sign
A Plus sign
A letter of the alphabet

A religious cross
A signature
A kiss
Two sticks
A cross road
Two swords for Sword Dance
A type of stitch
A sign to ward off evil
A mark of failure

A warning
String on a parcel
A water diviner
A tracking sign
A trellis
A coat rack
A jack from the side
A revolving door from above
A divider in a bottle carrier

Corners of adjoining rooms
Four States in USA
Points on the compass
A burnt Catherine Wheel
A spinning bobbin
A paper fortune teller
Four heads of mice touching nose

Suggested Answers

Pattern Detection

Exercise 1 – Party Games

1   words with double letters in them
2   words beginning with the last letter of the previous word
3   vertical and not horizontal
4   content not covering
5   above and not below

Exercise 2 – Cracking the Code

What is 42?   What is 23?

Exercise 3 – Ericksonian Riddles

Puzzle 1   gully, six, slip, bat, bowl = CRICKET
Puzzle 2   flags, float, March, Majorettes, brass band = A PARADE

Sorting Exercises

Exercise 2

Structure

- lengths of words
- number of words
- double letters
- foreign, English
- fonts and font size

Shapes

- circular, straight edged, curved
- size – small, large,
- symmetrical/asymmetrical

Function

- food, clothing, DIY, stationery
- items which connect, contain, cover, join, absorbed

Complexity

- part of something bigger, containing smaller parts

Misc

- words containing letters which score 8 and above in scrabble, score 4-8 points and score 1-3 points
- items with writing on them, and those without
- items which are attractive and those that aren't
- words which have more than one meaning

Exercise 3

Originator	Convertor	Deliverer
Farmer	Baker	Shop Assistant
Composer	Impresario	Conductor
Archaeologist	Museum Curator	Tour Guide
Geologist	Engineer	Constructor

Suggested Answers

Exercise 4

				The Structure
1.	A busy motorway interchange	A complex country dance	A tangled ball of string	There is always a clear pathway to follow
2.	Dress code	Disabled parking spaces	A shopping queue	Compliance
3.	A highly attractive physicist	A Shakespearian Play	A lively sports car	There is a lot under the bonnet
4.	A strawberry cream chocolate	An active volcano	A soft boiled egg	A soft runny centre
5.	Blowing up a balloon	A game of tenko – where you pull bricks out of a pile	Weighing sugar accurately	Finding the balance

There are of course other interpretations and common patterns that can be shared by these elements.

Exercise 5

Characteristics of a Potential Partner					
Appearance		Interpersonal		Personal	
Looks	Style	Social Behavior	Love Making	Mind	Emotional
5'7'-6' medium weight nice eyes lovely smile beautiful smile	smart casual good quality stylish fashionable	likes banter good conversatio-nalist enjoys people spends money thoughtfully likes variety	kind considerate unselfish passionate adventurous	quick witted rational logical intuitive well read	easy going holds his ground calm funny caring

Gathering Information

Asking Questions

Hitting the Target

Question 1: What would you rather have?

Outcome: To get to the Desired Outcome

- What would you like to have happen?
- If everything changed for the better, what would you be doing?
- If you could overcome all the obstacles, what would be happening?
- What is your ideal scenario?
- What do you secretly wish for?

Question 2: What's stopping you from doing this?

Outcome: To identify the limitations involved

- What is getting in the way of your success?
- What trips you up each time you try?
- What needs to be in place for it to work?
- What needs to be different?
- What has to happen to make it possible?

Question 3: What has to be true for this to be happening?

Outcome: To identify underlying beliefs

- What should you have been doing/not doing?
- What are you unable to do?

- What has led to this?
- What does this mean about you?
- What do you think others are thinking and saying?

Question 4: What do you fear might happen?

Outcome: To identify cause and effect beliefs

- What will this enevitably lead to?
- What is the downside to doing this?
- What is the worst that might happen?
- How might this end up?
- What do you really think is likely to happen?

Question 5: What is really important to you at the moment?

Outcome: To identify current operating value

- What would be disastrous if it happened?
- What are you paying attention to most?
- What must happen immediately or pretty soon?
- What would be the worst thing to happen now?
- Given all you believe about this, what now?

Finding The Question

Scenario 1

Rank		Reason
1	Q 5	The client seems to be presenting habitual behavior and is in a trance of same old, same old.
		This question provides a pattern disrupt. It offers a back track, places you firmly in the system and reminds your client of his purpose for being here. It causes your client to dissociate and view his own behavior clearly from 3rd position.
		It also presupposes that your client has resources of natural wisdom.
2	Q 3	This is another pattern disrupt. It presupposes that your client will often be 'doing their problem live' without knowing it. You can use what is happening now as a real illustration and unpack what is clearly evident for both of you to acknowledge.
3	Q 4	This question recognises existing confidence as a resource, and connects it with contemplating specifically the idea of exploring new ground.
4	Q 2	This question goes for secondary gain – a useful area of exploration when a stated outcome is not actually being pursued.
5	Q 1	This question addresses the implied Modal Operator of Necessity – the rule that might be inhibiting progress.

Scenario 2

Rank		Reason
1	Q 3	This Acting As If question presupposes that there are different styles of presenting and addresses any ecological issues that she may have. To answer this, she will have to conduct a TDS and discard all the styles that she recoils from and fears she might have to adopt if she is to be effective. Furthermore, to answer the question, she has to 'try on' each of the styles so creating a favourable reference experience for the one she chooses. It is a short step to then inviting her to fully explore this experience and test it in several different contexts. There is a phrase 'Fake it till you make it'.
2	Q 2	This solution focused question presupposes that she already has the resources and ways of managing her responses. When she is able to identify such times, you can build upon the resources within these reference experiences, strengthened by the counter examples, or else reveal the critical elements influencing the stronger responses.
3	Q 4	This question speeds up the Parts process by assuming that the need for protection is the issue, and generating alternative strategies. It also provides an embedded suggestion and a useful past referenced temporal predicate, supported by spatial marking of the Past.
4	Q 1	Here you are adopting a Partswork intervention which will commit you to your future line of question, which may or may not be appropriate.
5	Q 5	I suspect the client will have asked herself this lots of times and therefore not take her to new ground.

Scenario 3

Rank		Reason
1	Q 2	This is a massive reframe and pattern disrupt! Certainly cuts to the chase. Put like this, your client can only begin to question why she is still in a business relationship with this person. It challenges her holding onto respect and admiration in the face of the presenting evidence. In Sleight of Mouth terms, it is suggesting a different outcome than the presupposed one of 'getting better'.
2	Q 4	This question widens the system and shifts the roles and power dynamic. Helps your client explore other possibilities and causes of the current situation. Opens the possibility that it is not all down to her. Your client is not the problem.
3	Q 3	This could activate a strong listing of her own positive contribution to the business and therefore activating her own self-efficacy. Listing her own talents and resources breaks the imposed trance that she is responsible for current outcomes. Most likely quite the reverse.
4	Q 5	You are minimising the problem and indicating the cause. She is likely to have considered this already.
5	Q 1	This presupposes the problems lie with her relationship with her parents. Don't collude with the business partner.

Meta Model

Quiz

1b, 2a, 3a, 4c, 5c, 6b, 7c, 8a, 9c

Hidden Meta Model Patterns

1 **Modal Operator of Possibility**: Apart from the can't, won't, couldn't, wouldn't, watch out for the use of: impossible, difficult, unavoidable, unbearable, over-demanding, impregnable, restrictive, limited, untenable, intolerable

2 **Modal Operator of Necessity**: Apart from the must, ought, should, have to, watch out for the use of: essential, imperative, mandatory, critical, obligatory, crucial, vital, required, forbidden, illegal, frowned upon, prevented. And notice when 'I can't' is being used to mean 'I'm not allowed to'.

3 **Universal Quantifier**: Apart from the everybody, never, always, no-one, nobody, watch out for the use of: permanently, eternally, continuously, constantly, entirely, completely, totally, without fail, collective body, the team, the crowd, the mob, the company; collective groups: Scots, Asians, Left Handers, People with red hair.

4   **Lost Performative**: Apart from aphorisms, truisms, and proverbs, watch out for the use of: Everyone knows that… It's a given … It's a well known fact that … Research has shown … Traditionally … Generally … People who … You find that … Evidence suggests … It's generally accepted that … It's a commonly held view … Experience has proven that … It's plain to see that … It takes a discerning mind to … Only those and such as those … As a rule … .

5   **Mind Reading**: Apart from 'I know you think that …' watch out for the use of: You'll just love … You're bound to … They wont want to … He'll be delighted … She'll want much more … They will really appreciate this … This will make all the difference … He doesn't mean it … He was having you on … I suspect you … .

6   **Cause and Effect**: Apart from 'this leads to that', watch out for the use of: It figures… doomed, fated, desirable/ undesirable consequences, not worth the risk… powerless, inevitable, automatic, programmed, mindless, preordained, inescapable, foretold, a given.

7   **Complex Equivalence**: Apart from 'this means that', and two apparently disconnected statements, watch out for the use of: symptomatic, symbolises, typical, indicates, implies, denotes, represents, epitomises, typifies, boils down to, signifies, otherwise, or else.

What to Go For – Suggested Answers

Example 1

I always end up badly in negotiations. I've become really nervous and now my reputation has suffered.

   U   UV   N   CE   MR   N   CE

I don't have the killer instinct that this job seems to demand. I always end up badly in negotiations. I've become really nervous and now my reputation has suffered. But I don't want to be one of those hardened, screw 'em type of guys. I can't see why we can't go for a win:win outcome

Fran: I would go for the Lost Performative – Who says (all) negotiators are hardened people? Followed by questioning the Universal of All negotiators. This will address the undesirable Cause and Effect.

Example 2

This is blissful! Everyone should love this, or else they have no soul!

   LRI   U   MON   MR   CEQ

I can't stand those people who turn their nose up at a bit of luxury and make out that they are somehow superior.   This is blissful! Everyone should love this, or else they have no soul!

Fran: I may tackle the Complex Equivalence. 'What's the connection between whatever "it" is and "soul"?' since it may widen perceptual positions. Then I would go for the mind reading and the universal of 'them' thinking they are superior.

Example 3

That suggestion is out of the question. It's totally disrespectful to expect us to respond in this manner! I feel quite insulted.

   LRI   N   MOP/MON   U   CEQ   LRI   CE

We have provided them with all the information. We have answered their endless queries and now they are suggesting that we now become part of a tendering process. That suggestion is out of the question. It's totally disrespectful to expect us to respond in this manner! I feel quite insulted. I have a good mind to contact the CEO tell her that we are withdrawing from the whole process.

Fran: I would go for the Cause and Effect – Suggestion➔ Feeling Insulted, since this will open up more nested beliefs.

Example 4

I feel a failure. I should have done more to keep my marriage alive.

   CEQ   MON   UV   SD   CE

I feel a failure. I should have done more to keep my marriage alive. My husband says it is nothing to do with me, just that he wants different things. He even said that he knew he shouldn't have married me at the time! But there must be something wrong with me, that I'm not enough for him.

Fran: I would go for Cause and Effect – Marriage ending ➔Personal Failure and follow if up with an exploration of Lost Performatives around failure.

Frames and Reframes

Purpose of the Outcome Elements

1 **State the Outcome Positively**: Often when you ask somebody what they want, they will tell you more about those things that they do not want. It is worthwhile spending time in this area in order to establish the outcome in positive terms. If you are concentrating on what you do not want – then that is likely to be what you get. You may have heard of the consideration that our unconscious mind doesn't work with negative commands. We have to have a representation of the thing we mustn't do, or don't want, to make sense of the injunction. This is why it is much more useful to have a sign that reads 'Place all rubbish in bins provided' as opposed to 'Don't drop litter'.

2 **Establish the Level of Value**: The motivation to achieve the outcome will be relative to the importance that individual has, or purpose that the individual is running. Outcomes will be strongly held if they are consciously or unconsciously linked to our life purpose and mission. In fact, what is the purpose of such an outcome if it isn't! It may be that an outcome is an expedient and an indirect means to an end. If it is then it is important that this is recognised.

   If the outcome is not held at a high value, then either it is a waste of time literally, or is likely to be someone else's value that has been taken on. If the outcome is not valued, then the explorer will fall at the first signs of adversity and setback.

3 **Put the Outcome into Context**: This is important particularly if the outcome involves a change in behaviour. Check when it is appropriate to have the outcome. One reason for putting off pursuing an outcome is the belief that we have to take all of it on, all of the time, starting from now. Realising that we can be selective ups the level of commitment to a particular course of action.

4 **Identify Evidence:** We need to recognise when we've achieved what we want. Otherwise we may discover we have it without realising it. This is Exit part of the TOTE. The evidence needs to be sensory specific, so that we can have a reference experience of achieving it. This informs our unconscious mind of our desired goal and it filters incoming information accordingly, alerting us when we get closer, or further away, from the end point. Asking to go second position provides an early ecology check as well, since we can decide if we like what we see. If we don't, we can make early adjustments, or else we can pinpoint what has been holding us back.

5 **Own Outcome Personally**: Often we place the responsibility for our outcomes onto others, which means not only that we leave ourselves open to being dependent on actions which may never happen, but also we avoid taking full responsibility for the work. It is also important that we gain some insight into what has led to previous inability to attain this outcome. If we always do what we have always done, we'll always get what we've always got. So it is important to be clear, in advance, of what we are going to do differently.

6 **Resources:** Success requires a strategy, and it is essential to ensure that we marshal the necessary resources around us, proactively. These resources may be people, skills, money, time, materials, energy, goodwill, and momentum. Sometimes we may need to establish an interim outcome which deals with bringing these resources within our sphere of influence. Without javing them to hand, we may find ourselves stretched and stranded.

7 **Check the Ecology**: Often we might say we want such and such, but when we really think about it, we may actually want something different. This might be because the outcome is past its sell-by date. Or it is an outcome favoured by another – father, teacher, friend. Or it may be something that we think we ought to want, to fit in. The ecology check really tests the internal congruence signals that come from our internal parts. If this signal is not listened to and over-ridden, then the outcome will be sabotaged sooner than later. Our inner wisdom beats our conscious mind any day!

8 **Place into the Future**: Looking from a future position, when this outcome has been achieved, it helps to seal the outcome into a reality. It puts today's wish into tomorrow's achievements. It lends perspective to today's decision. It also tests the viability and comfort of the outcome – its 'rightness', and again it offers instructions to the unconscious mind. From this perspective, it is easier to be clear about what to do and when.

What's Been Offered?

What's been offered	What to usefully explore
Clear Evidence of Dad's response Value implied but not confirmed Setbacks possibly offering the needed resource of feedback, but not confirmed.	Outcome more a wish than anything else. Ideally looking for: I want to get this job.
	Need to clarify value to make sure it is not father's outcome and is in fact hers.
	Context not clarified, although the wider conversation may be about approaching interview.
	No clear statement of what has to be done differently, or how the setback.

Positive outcome Value of 'being somebody' Context Resources Evidence measured by turnover	Ecology question – Does he really want everyone to 'sit up and listen?' Does he have any reservations about this. Contribution – need to clarify what has held him back. No evidence for 'sit up and listen'.
Value of being fulfilled Context – by 40	Remedy expressed. Need to know what 'something worthwhile' will bring. Evidence not clear. Resources not clear. Contribution not clear. Ecology not clear. On closer inspection it may be she wants out of her marriage.
Positive outcome – though a specifiedst 1st or 2.1 may be significant Value – worth the work Evidence – of a degree but not necessarily a 'good' one Contribution hinted at Resources – hard work and life balance	Evidence – may need to nail evidence more specifically e.g. see document with the result written down, or hear name and degree called out. Need to clarify what she is going to be doing differently.

Obscure Outcomes

Action	What is my Secondary Gain?	What is my Positive Intention?
Getting poor results at college	Feeding a belief that I am not good enough Avoiding being found out	To protect myself from disappointment and disapproval.
Turning down invitations to go on foreign holidays	Saving money	To stay safe within familiar worlds, and not showing myself up.
Eating too much	Gaining favour with my partner who does all the cooking Opportunity to eat just what I like	To avoid being asked out so I am safe. To avoid sex.
Not settling down into a permanent relationship	Keeping lots of options open. Getting a chance to visit and meet lots of different people	To avoid commitment and intimacy.

PRO Frame

P R O?	Which is which?	Question
O	I am motivated and enthusiastic.	And if you got that, would you want it?
R	We want to be recognised.	And when you're recognised, then what happens?
R	I want to be more effective.	And when you're more effective, then what happens?
R	I want to feel optimistic.	And when you're optimistic, then what happens?
O	We want to win the Best Team Award.	And if you got that would you want it?
R	I want to be less negative.	And when you are less negative, then what happens?
O	I am a good decision maker.	And if you got that would you want it?
P	We are overlooked.	What would you like to have happen?
P	I do the same things time and again.	What would you like to have happen?

Suggested Answers

General Frames

Situation	Frame
1 is confused and doesn't trust his thinking.	As If Frame
2 has at least two options both of which seem fairly attractive.	Contrast Frame
3 has just gone through a fairly rambling account, and has paused for breath.	Backtrack Frame
4 has gone off on a tangent, after you asked a specific meta model question.	Relevancy Challenge
5 keeps saying 'I don't know' when you are asking 'Whereabouts is that feeling?'	As If Frame
6 has offered four possible causal outcomes based on Lost Performatives and Mind Readings.	Backtrack Frame
7 has mentioned an ex partner frequently when discussing her current relationship?	Contrast Frame
8 has begun to tell a story when you've asked 'What would you like to have happen?'	Relevancy Challenge
9 has introduced two seemingly disconnected stories, considering the subject that you were talking about.	Relevancy Challenge
10 finds it difficult to say what he thinks the consequences might be.	As If Frame

Integration

Deconstructing Language

Exercise 1

- What was surprising you about your performance?
- How did you manage that?
- What beliefs and values were influencing your decision-making?

Presuppositions	Q1	Personal performances can bring surprises. That there were situations that could generate surprises. That the individual was capable of being surprised. That this was an on-going process.
	Q2	That you are responsible for your own surprise. That you made it happen through your own actions.
	Q3	That beliefs and values influence decision making. That what you did to surprise yourself was because of decisions you took. What you believe supports your ability to be surprised.
Timeframe	Q1	Attention to activities throughout an unspecified period of time (probably previous day).
	Q2	Attention placed on that time period.
	Q3	Attention on specific thinking processes during the previous day.
Transderivational Search		Surprising events related to own performance
		Looking at the process and abilities involved in the act of becoming surprised. So accessing those moments that were not anticipated or habitual.
		What decisions had been taken? What led up to those decisions? What meaning had been put onto those events?
Meta Model	Q1	Cause – Effect: what generates surprise.
		Modal Operator of Necessity: what has to happen to become surprised.
	Q2	Unspecified Verb: the process of managing.
	Q3	Cause-Effect: beliefs lead to influencing decision making.
Neurological Level		Behaviour – being surprised. Capability – ability to do something different, self manage and make decisions. Beliefs and Values – in support of decision making within performance.
Meta Message		You can surprise yourself! You can take yourself out of your habitual patterns and give yourself new information about yourself You are in charge.
Outcome		To confirm that you can bring newness into your world through your own actions

Exercise 2

- What is continually delighting you?
- What does this tell you about your Purpose?
- What will be the significance of that?

Presuppositions	Q1	You are being delighted. It is an on-going process. Learning and learning context can delight.
	Q2	There is a connection between delight and Purpose. You have a Purpose.
	Q3	Knowing your Purpose and evidence of it has a significance that will be significant at some future time.
Timeframe	Q1	Attention to being part of an on-going process extending beyond today and this weekend.
	Q2	Attention on current internal dialogue.
	Q3	Attention on future future future time: 1) 'will be' – future, 2) 'significance' – a retrospective evaluation, 3) 'that' – further dissociation pushing further into future.

Transderivational Search	Scanning sources of delight which are recurring, so identifying a pattern.
	Accessing understanding of Purpose and linking this with delight. Testing the connection between the two. Making connections between the sources and Purpose.
	Future rehearsing the effects of connecting actions with Purpose and what such a life might be like.
Meta Model	Q1/2 Cause – Effect: events/actions lead to delight lead to connection with Purpose.
	Q3 Complex Equivalence: connecting with Purpose is significant.
Neurological Level	Behaviour: Actions generating delight. Values: Delight. Spiritual: Purpose.
Meta Message	What you do to delight yourself directly connects you to your Purpose. Seek delight.
Outcome	To discover how delighting in learning can fuel your greater Purpose in life.

Exercise 3

- What has been drawing your attention and interest?
- How might this compare with the experiences of others?
- What could this say about you as a Learner?

Presuppositions	Q1 Your attention and interest has been drawn, by something. That you have been motivated towards and not away from, from use of metaphor 'drawing'.
	Q2 There are others around, who may have been sharing the same events, and who may have similar or different experiences to you. You have the ability to second position.
	Q3 Comparison can provide information. This information is related to learning. The use of 'could' implies that there may be more than one complex equivalence to be had.
Timeframe	Q1 Attention to on going recent events.
	Q2 Attention to present comparison with recent past of others.
	Q3 Attention on close future.
Transderivational Search	Scanning range of events which attracted and intrigued.
	Imagining the experiences of others from their perspective and forming a comparison.
	From the collation of this meta information, scanning the inferences of it in connection with you and learning.
Meta Model	Q1 Simple Deletion: object of attraction and curiosity.
	Q2 Unspecified Verb: process of comparison with others.
	Modal Operator of Possibility: use of might.
	Q3 Complex Equivalence: comparison content means you are a certain type of learner.
Neurological Level	Behaviour: being drawn. Beliefs: comparisons meaning X as a learner.
Perspective	Second positioning others
Meta Message	You are open to being attracted and intrigued. Others may have similar or different experiences to you. Learning can come from the feedback from comparisons.
Outcome	To demonstrate our uniqueness as a learner. To learn from other learners.

Exercise 4

- Knowing what you know now, and having the skills you can now draw on, how will this assist your learning today?
- And how else?

Presuppositions	Q1 You know what you now know. You know the skills you now have and that you can draw on them. 'Now' implies skills and knowledge have been building. Such skills and knowledge contribute to learning, specifically today.
	Q2 That there is more to consider than you have thought so far.
	Q3 There is a reason for this cause and effect.

Timeframe	Q1	Attention from previous ongoing activity to present time and into future time framed within today
	Q2	Attention on same time frame.
	Q3	Attention present.
Transderivational Search	Collation of new knowledge and skills, contrasted with what existed previously. Expectations of the day's events and mapping new knowledge and skills to these events. Scanning reasons behind these cause and effects, based on previous occasions.	
Meta Model	Q1	Cause-Effect: knowledge and skills leads to assisting learning.
Milton Model	Phonological Ambiguity: your learning / you are learning.	
Neurological Level	Capability: knowledge and skills; process of learning.	
Meta Message	You have been learning. You are a proven learner. You will be continuing your learning.	
Outcome	To bring you into your conscious competence as a Learner.	

Exercise 5

- What is guaranteed to inspire you as a learner?
- What does this say about you?
- How does this affect your relationship with learning?

Presuppositions	Q1	You become inspired in learning. Certain things will always inspire you. Learning is a given. Inspiration is possible.
	Q2	That you can infer meaning from this. That you and others have an opinion about this.
	Q3	This opinion can influence how you relate to learning.
Timeframe	Q1	Attention to through time: 'is' present, 'guaranteed' past, 'to inspire' future facing.
	Q2	Attention on present.
	Q3	Attention on present to future: 'affect'.
Transderivational Search	Scanning for patterns of what triggers Inspirational responses to events. Scanning internal dialogue from self and others by way of meta comment. Clarifying relationship with learning and viewing with this insight.	
Meta Model	Q1	Universal Quantifier: 'guaranteed'.
	Q2	Lost Performative: unseen opinion giver.
	Q3	Unspecified Verb: the process of being affected.
		Cause and Effect and Lost Performative: Influences relationship.
		Nominalisation: Relationship.
Neurological Level	Value: 'inspire'. Belief: cause and effects.	
Perspectives	Third position viewing relationship of you and learning.	
Meta Message	You have patterns of inspiration. These can define your identity. Your relationship with learning can change	
Outcome	To focus attention on what motivates, and what you want to ask for as a learner.	

Suggested Answers

Exercise 6

- What have you been noticing about your learning?
- What would you rather have?
- How will this have been of more benefit to you and others?

Presuppositions	Q1	You've been thinking about your learning and noticing some things. That the focus is on l earning and not what is being learned.
	Q2	That what you're doing or getting is not enough. That you want more.
	Q3	That you are achieving something different that could benefit you and others.
Timeframe	Q1	Attention to recent past.
	Q2	Attention on possible future.
	Q3	Attention on effects in future 'will', future 'have been'.
Transderivational Search		Scanning all neurological levels of learning Scanning for what has come above threshold and into attention.
		Scanning for what is missing and desirable. Scanning for the future impact of alternative benefits.
Meta Model	Q1	Simple Deletion: retrieving object of noticing.
	Q2	Comparative Deletion: 'rather'.
	Q3	Comparative Deletion: 'more'.
Milton Model		Non Sensory Verb: 'noticing'.
		Phonological Ambiguity: your learning / you are learning.
		Permission: 'might'.
Perspective		Second positioning others to ascertain benefits.
Outcome Frame		Contrast Frame: 'What would you rather have?'
		Value of Outcome: benefit to you and others.
		Ecology Check: to establish if such benefits a) exist b) are beneficial.
Neurological Level		Behaviour: 'noticing'. Beliefs and Values: nature of benefits
Meta Message		You have choice about your learning, at all levels. You don't have to accept what you have. You need to consider benefits.
Outcome		To wake up from your habitual learning trance and establish an explicit outcome.

Exercise 7

- How have you been restricting your learning?
- How has this been serving you?
- How might others have described that?

Presuppositions	Q1	That you have been restricting yourself. That restrictions can be self imposed. That you can learn more. It is down to you.
	Q2	That there is a secondary gaine to this limitation and you have been holding on to it.
	Q3	That there are other ways of looking at this.
Timeframe	Q1	Attention to learning activities over time.
	Q2	Attention on this action taking place through time in the past.
	Q3	Attention further into the past – through past tense and 'that'.
Transderivational Search		Looking for instances of limitation. Evaluating personal contribution. Scanning for the benefits. Imagined or real responses from others in the past

Suggested Answers

Meta Model	Q1 Unspecified Verb: process of 'restricting'. Cause-Effect: actions lead to limited learning. Q2 Unspecified Verb: process of 'serving'. Complex Equivalence: limitations means existence of positive intention.
Neurological Level	Capability: ability to restrict, ability to know what others may think. Beliefs: understanding secondary gain.
Perspective	Second position others.
Reframing	Higher Value: positive intention. Model of the World: the views of others.
Meta Programme	Move away from the negative thoughts of others. Move towards feeling better about self. External Referencing.
Meta Message	You are in charge of your learning. You influence the responses of others.
Outcome	To loosen the hold existing limitations have been placing on your learning.

Exercise 8

- What unexpected success did you have?
- How did you make this happen?
- How will this be important in your everyday work?

Presuppositions	Q1 That you were successful. It was unexpected. You limit your expectations. Q2 That you were responsible for this outcome. You can create the unexpected. You can extend your scope of success. Q3 are That your self determination can be transferred. That you can be more successful. That you in control of the outcomes you achieve.
Timeframe	Q1 Attention on (the previous day). Q2 Attention on (previous day,) brought nearer into the present with 'this' Q3 Attention from present 'this' to future, through time.
Transderivational Search	Scanning for successes, even the smallest, in the unexpected category. Awareness of what expected success is like. Question what has to happen to make them unexpected. Discover skills and behaviours that made the difference. Explore beliefs which restrict success and those which open up the potential for success. Scanning for when limiting beliefs didn't serve at work, and those situations where this new thinking could be usefully applied. Reference experience of future success.
Meta Model	Q1 Unspecified Verb: the process of being unexpectedly successful Q3 Complex Equivalence: knowing this success will be subsequently important
Reframe	Success was down to you, not some Act of God.
Perspective	Full Association with the pegging of 'this', so maintaining the anchor of the reference experience.
Neurological Level	Behaviour: being successful. Capability: ability to extend and transfer self efficacy. Beliefs: what is important at work.
Meta Message	You are more than you think you are. The more you understand about your abilities the more effective you can be. You have reference experiences to draw on and resource you.
Outcome	To develop self belief in own abilities.

Technology

Techniques

Purposes of the CommonTechniques

	Purpose	Calibration Evidence
6 Step Reframe	To remove an unwanted behaviour	No objections from other Parts. Ability to view suggested behaviour in the future.
Change Personal History	To remove an undesirable state	Past memory no longer triggers old response.
Circle of Excellence	To develop a resourceful state	Resourceful state appears when anchor is fired in reality or in imagination.
Disney Strategy	To create a viable dream	The Critic has no more to say.
Meta Mirror	To find a resourceful response to an unsatisfactory relationship	There is no sign of the physiology of initial first position.
Neurological Level Alignment	To strengthen Identity within a specific environment To generate a powerful resource state and anchor	On return to the Environment, there is a significant shift in the submodalities from the original inventory.
New Behaviour Generator	To generate viable alternative behaviours	Full congruence when associated into the preferred behaviour.
Phobia 'Cure'	To remove a phobic response	No phobic response when original triggers are fired.

SCORE	To clarify stuck situation and identify the appropriate resources to generate change	A realistic Action Plan with identified resources. Heightened energy and motivation. (Dancing the SCORE)The movement is fluid and grounded. Physiology of Cause is hard to access.
Swish	To remove an unwanted habit	Old trigger no longer fires the unwanted behaviour.
Timeline Alignment	To create a balanced relationship between Past, Present and Future	Balance in Present, with holding and nudge from Past, pull from Future.
Visual Squash	To resolve inner conflict	Internal calm and expression of hope.

Components within a Technique

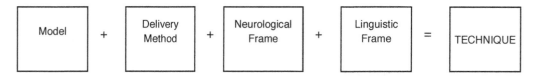

Labelling the Elements

Dreamer, Realist, Critic; Power, Control, Vulnerability, Safety,;Tender, Fierce, Playful

Skills for Technique Delivery

Skill	Importance
Linguistic Delivery	Your voice acts as an anchor, a means of directing state and resourcing, of directing inner attention.
Second Positioning	It is essential that you are responsive to what is happening with the explorer and not the technique or yourself. Your decisions regarding your flexibility start from the feedback you gain here.
Responding to Own Incongruence	Personal congruence is essential to build up a trusting relationship and transmit confidence to the explorer.
Paying Attention to Ecology	You are in a highly responsible position and have to act with absolute integrity.
Sensory Acuity	Everything you do and say will be determined by the responses you are getting – provided you notice them.
Maintaining Rapport	You are inviting an explorer to enter into unknown inner territory, previously unexplored. This asks for confidence and possibly courage from the explorer. If your levels of rapport are not sufficiently strong, the explorer is unlikely to follow your leads.
Overcoming Resistance	Provided your outcome, i.e. the explorer's outcome, is ecological and well formed, resistance is information that you need to do something different. This requires steady pacing before any leading.
Managing Space	Techniques involving spatial anchors require a finite amount of space. It is your job to ensure that you mark out the space you have available sufficiently for the explorer to access discrete states.

Suggested Answers

Managing Time	You need ot know how long a technique will take, and decide on the hoof if you need to cut bits out, or change the delivery method. Or recontract with your explorer(s).
Positioning	You have to be outside of your explorer's energy field so that he/she is free to fully explore the space around. And you must be meticulous about not treading on established anchors.
Resourcing	The explorer needs to feel free and trusting to continue exploring. It is your job to keep them buoyant whilst respecting their inner processing. Timing regarding intervention is critical.
Multiple Attending	You need to keep track of events over multiple systems. If stuck go meta and evaluate what is happening.
Managing Process	You need to have a firm hand on the process of the technique, otherwise you will end up somewhere else. You are in charge of the process, not the explorer.
Anchoring and Marking Out	It is essential that through your voice and gestures you reinforce the hallucinated reality created by the exemplar and/or the layout of the spatial anchors.
Sponsoring	You are sponsoring your explorer and so have to be Tender, Fierce and Playful to keep your explorer at optimum resourcefulness.
Being Flexible	It is your call regarding when you depart from the set procedures and introduce something else; or when you move out to a dissociated position; or adopt Fierce as opposed to Tender; or construct your own questions. Imagine each time you have an invisible supervisor in the corner of the room and you have to be accountable for your decision making!

Logistics of Time

1   True – NLL Alignment is ¾ hour to do, whilst 6 Step Reframe is about 15 mins.

2   True – an elegant practitioner will take less time than one who is currently merely effective.

3   True – It is quicker when an explorer just goes with what plops as opposed to thinking about the answer.

4   False – not relevant.

5   False – the nature of the problem is not relevant. The structure determines the process.

6   False – as above.

7   True – an 'inexperienced' explorer may need more reassurance.

8   True – a small chunker takes longer.

9   True – resistance takes time to overcome.

10 True – and these can't be anticipated.

11 True – though perhaps detrimentally. If the practitioner is well versed in the process then they will be fluent and not need to refer to notes. They may also run the risk of deleting and so shortening the time involved.

12 True – additional time requirements need to be factored into the decision to deviate from the set procedure.

13 True – content free approaches save loads of time. Your explorer might need to hear their thoughts out loud which makes for doubling or more the time requirements.

14 True – if time is short then you could select a different approach whilst keeping to the technique.

15 True – it's your call to remove elements within a technique – consciously. You need to be aware of what will be lost as well as the time gains.

16 True – you may have an explorer who cannot physically stand for the length of time required by the technique. You may need to find another way of delivering it.

17 False – generally speaking. However, there may be some resistance and therefore time taken up if the explorer has had a bad experience with that approach previously.

18 True – putting yourself and your explorer under pressure to complete within a time limit usually adds to the length of time taken.

Suggested Answers

Selection of Interventions

Scenario 1 – Jane

Neurological Level Alignment: This would be appropriate because the process will strengthen her Identity as a Presenter, connect her to a wider personal system, give her Mentors to support and resource her, rehearse positively what to do and the skills she needs, and give her a profound reference experience to draw on when the time comes.

Phobia 'Cure': You could consider her response to be phobic. Dissociating her involuntary kinaesthetic from her past experience may well do it. This may address behaviours but not identity.

Scenario 2 – Mike

Meta Mirror: not with his Line Manager, though that could be useful. Instead with the person who originally bullied him in his childhood. It may have been a parent, sibling, or teacher. This dissociation process can stretch the system to generate new responses and internal resources to equip him in his subsequent dealings with his boss.

New Behaviour Generator: You could coach him to rehearse various ways of handling his boss in future situations, which would be helpful. But since this is a fairly superficial behavioural solution, it might not combat his default position of emotional impotence.

Scenario 3 – Asif

Visual Squash: This is a clear case of two Parts in conflict, with the resultant push/pull. By developing a third Part equipped to take him through the bind he is in, he will be likely to maintain his relationship with his family whilst securing the future he wants.

Circle of Excellence: You could coach him into developing the Resource that he needs to state his case with his parents, making sure that you fully test for ecology. But an enhanced resource state doesn't necessarily recognise the positive intentions of both Parts and honour his full system.

Scenario 4 – Honour

Timeline Alignment: Worry is a Future based emotion, suggesting that not much time is spent fully in the Present. At the same time, there is a history of anxiety, suggesting that the Past is not supportive either. By clearing out her relationship with time, and securing a full flow of energy throughout, the explorer will gain a different relationship with her Future and her Present.

Swish: You could identify a scenario when she is not anxious and establish a submodality profile and compare this with the submodalities of an anxious scenario. You could then substitute the positive profile into the anxious state, and use this as the positive Swish image. This would address the issue of anxiety, but not achieve the overall 'cleansing' that the alignment process would achieve.

Technique Components

Models

Quiz

1a, 2a, 3a, 4c, 5b, 6c, 7c, 8a, 9b, 10c, 11b, 12a, 13a, 14c, 15a

Labelling of Elements

1 **Critic, Creator, Planner, Dreamer:** Creator and Dreamer are duplications, and Dreamer is nearer in level to Critic. Planner is only part of the Realist process and should be upgraded to Realist.

2 **Dreamlike, Planning, Criticism:** The three labels are all of different types. Criticism is a noun, Dreamlike an adjective and Planning is a verb. They need to be all of the same.

3 **Look Up, To Do List, Criticism:** The elements are at different logical levels, at different levels of complexity. Again we have a nominalisation with Criticism, a verb To Look Up and another different form of noun with the To Do List.

4 **Be receptive, Dream, Have Ideas; Receive ideas, Identify resources, Make plans; Evaluate plans, Find problems, Ask questions:** Here is a classic over complication! It is likely the modeller has lost sight of the end purpose. This model's redeeming feature is that all the elements are verbs, which is something, but we know that chunking up to Dreamer Realist Critic, renders the model tight and succinct. The individual elements can be further unpacked should the modeller or acquisition designer so choose.

Accepted Labelling: Dreamer, Realist, Critic

5 **Powerful, Controlling, Safely, Vulnerability:** Again here is an adjective, adjective, noun, noun. The whole model becomes tight when each element is expressed in the same format.

6 **Impotent, Over controlled, Unsafe, Impregnable:** This time we have possible outcomes for each of the elements, again not following the same pattern. Currently it is the extreme understrength, extreme overstrength, extreme understrength, and extreme overstrength. As a model it could work if it were all over strengths or all understrength.

7 **Powerless, Controlled, Safety, Vulnerability:** Another mish-mash. Powerless is a 'negative' whilst the others are neutral or positive – depending on viewpoint. Controlled is a verb and the other two are nominalisations.

Accepted Labelling: Power, Control, Safety, Vulnerability

8 **Tenderness, Fierce, Playfulness:** Tenderness and Playfulness are nominalisations and Fierce is an adjective. Again needs to be consistently one or the other.

9 **Tender, Fiercely, Playing:** All over the place: adjective, adverb and continuous verb.

10 **The Queen, The King, The Jester:** This works as the archetype descriptions of Tender, Fierce, Playful.

Accepted Labelling: Tender, Fierce, Playful

Name the Types of Models

No	Category	Type	No	Category	Type
1	Constructed	Hierarchical	6	Constructed	Tabular
2	Constructed	Simultaneous	7	Constructed	Sequential
3	Constructed	Tabular	8	Idiosyncratic	Illustrative
4	Idiosyncratic	Illustrative	9	Constructed	Simultaneous
5	Constructed / Core	Hierarchical / Complex	10	Constructed	Tabular

Suggested Answers

Labelling the Elements

| | Nominalisation | Verb | | Adjective | Part/Archetype |
		Present	'ing' verb		
1	Appreciation	Appreciate	Appreciating	Appreciative	The Fan
2	Tenacity	Be tenacious	Being Tenacious	Tenacious	The Athlete
3	Connection	Connect	Connecting	Connective	The Link
4	Compassion	Be Compassionate	Being Compassionate	Compassionate	The Carer
5	Talents	Be Talented	Being Talented	Talented	The Genius
6	Fun	Be funny	Being Funny	Funny	The Joker
7	Curiosity	Be curious	Being Curious	Curious	The Seeker
8	Reflection	Reflect	Reflecting	Reflective	The Thinker
9	Promotion	Promote	Promoting	Promotional	The Promoter
10	Protection	Protect	Protecting	Protective	The Guard
11	Socialisation	Socialise	Socialising	Social	The Socialiser
12	Commitment	Commit	Committing	Commited	The Determiner

Delivery Methods

Scenario 1

You've been given written notes on Bill O'Hanlon's Blissed, Blessed, Pissed, Dissed model in tabular form. You have 1.5 hours to include a demonstration. The group is creative and adventurous, Proximity, Feeling and Move Towards.

1   **Somatic Syntax:** Given the profile of the group I would go for this rather avantgarde, physical approach asking them to adopt different physiology for each element and combining them to deliver a predetermined goal. This would be pairs exercise. The model doesn't imply causal, hierarchical or relationship between the elements, so you may need to get the explorer to choose the location of each of the elements.

2   **Card Sort:** If there is additional information supporting each of the elements, then creating a cardsort and inviting your explorers to create a meaningful structure out of the cards could be a useful way of enabling a familiarity with the framework and an overall understanding of the dynamic.

3   **Visual Diagram:** You could ask individuals to plot the occurrence of each element through time for emerging themes.

Scenario 2

You've been given Prochaska's sequential Change model, with a description of each stage. You have the slot after lunch. The group is Collaborative, Proactive, and Move Away From.

1   **Spatial Anchors + Sound:** I would involve a physical activity requiring groups of 5 if possible, with one person taking responsibility for an element. Working with the Move Away from, have each person identify want they want to avoid in each of these stages, working with temporal predicates.

2   **Spatial Anchors:** This could be a straightforward spatial pairs exercise which will come alive with the addition of neurological frames. This may be less threatening and/or more meaningful for individuals. It also doesn't rely on the creativity or time required coming up with the 'instruments'.

3   **Story:** Allocate each element to individuals in groups of 5, either as a goldfish bowl exercise or in separate groups. Identify a topic, or it could be a real situation for someone present. Each individual tells their part of the story around that element, or starts a story and passes it on to the next person for the next element to continue.

Suggested Answers

Scenario 3

The group has identified that Trust is lacking in their team. They have come up with three components which they consider contributes directly to levels of Trust – Respect, Commitment, Acceptance.

1. **Sliding Scales:** Ask each person to identify other Team Members one by one, and establish where their own levels for each component for each relationship are. And then explore what it would be like altering the levels until they become acceptably strong. The second part could be to have members face each other and walk towards each other until the midpoint has been reached for each component – 'meeting people half way'.

2. **Guided Visualisation + Confusion Technique:** Whilst you could use spatial anchors or a written exercise, you could provide the group with a trance inducing visualisation as they explore Respectful Acceptance, Acceptable Respect, Respectful Commitment, Committed Respect, Accepting Commitment, Commited Acceptance.

3. **Spatial Anchors:** Working alone and selecting one particular team member where the relationship is poor, work each space with this person in mind. Again the neurological frames will bring this alive.

Scenario 4

You are now at the last 10 minutes of the session. You have been exploring with your client her responses to conflict and in the process she realises that she has a distinct ambivalence about her abilities and desire to confront. There will be a follow on session, so you want her to leave in a strong resourceful state

1. **Binary Hands:** Allocate Not Wanting Conflict and Wanting Conflict, one to either hand. Allow the hands to work their own process until they come to rest.

2. **Stories/Readings:** Offer stories you may have about conflict, or readings and poems that you may already have up your sleeve for such a common issue. Identify metaphors which isomorphically match this issue – dams and reservoirs, theatrical masks. Invite your client to identify specific metaphors which reflect her situation. Then task her to go out and find physical examples of these metaphors and bring back her thoughts on them for the next session.

3. Develop a process which is a pure combination of neurological frames supported by selected linguistic frames.

Scenario 5

You have McWhirter's hierarchical Performance, Management, Direction and Supervision model, which you know is quite impactful and deserves quality time given to it. You want to do something different and memorable. And it might serve to round off a day's training, or help dislodge a client's stuck state.

1. **Guided Visualisation + Drawing:** As part of the closing of the session, take your group or individual up through the stages, spending time at the summit before anchoring and coming back down again to the present. The explorer could then draw a description of whatever they experienced.

2. **Questions**: Construct a series of questions which reflects the dynamics of each of the elements and, content free in pairs, have the explorer work through each of the stages. At the end, there may be a message for them which again you could get them to write and illustrate.

3. **Spatial Anchors:** The group, as a body, could step back through the stages as directed, and come back with an anchored experience. This approach can be effective, but it obviously cannot accommodate indvidual's needs. You could back this up with a worksheet with the questions you were using and so individual responses could be captured.

Scenario 6

You have a coaching client you have been seeing for some time. Change is happening. He has now fully recognised the issues which are holding him back and is currently exploring how he might deal with life without his habitual behaviour patterns. You have strong rapport with him. You feel your sessions may have become stale and you want to break the trance.

1. **Somatic Syntax:** Combine different physiologies through time from the start of the process through to successful resolution. Once established join them together so that they form one free flowing movement. Invite him to pay particular attention the the transition between now and the next step.

2. **Spatial Anchors**: this scenario lends itself to some imaginative use of neurological frames.

3. **Questions**: You could come up with a series of laser questions incorporating key linguistic patterns to provoke new awareness.

Neurological Frames

Quiz Answers

1c , 2a, 3c, 4b, 5b, 6c, 7a, 8b, 9a, 10a, 11a, 12b, 13a, 14a, 15b, 16c, 17c, 18b, 19a, 20b, 21c, 22a, 23b, 24b

Do you know your techniques?

	VAK	Submodalities	Time	Multiple Perspective	Space Associated/Dissociated	Metaphor	Mentors	Parts/Archetypes	Anchoring
6 Step Reframe								✔	
Change Personal History			✔		✔				✔
Circle of Excellence		✔			✔				✔
Disney Strategy								✔	✔
Meta Mirror				✔	✔			✔	✔
Neurological Level Alignment	✔	✔	✔	✔		✔	✔		✔
New Behaviour Generator	✔				✔				
Phobia 'Cure'		✔		✔					
SCORE					✔	✔			✔
Swish					✔				✔
Timeline Alignment		✔			✔	✔			✔
Visual Squash	✔								✔

What might you get?

These are suggested answers. If they differ from your own, that doesn't automatically mean you are off the mark, just that there is more to reflect upon. We are living with an imprecise science here, and this exercise is entering into the realms of art. However, the neurological frames do have a specific contribution to make, and it is these that you want to be certain of.

1   You would be able to gain a three dimensional description of the state, and discover how the structure changes when the state intensifies or diminishes. You could plot the shifts in state through time, as described by the variance in submodality configuration.

2   You would save 20 minutes! And you would reduce the range of information available to inform the process and deepen the association into it.

3   You could either 'grow' You and The Other, to discover how the grown up You would tackle The Other today. It is likely that there will be a point when The Other ceases to be dominating, or intimidating. This might not have the same power to alter any of the beliefs that may have formed at the early event.

4   You wouldn't have anything to calibrate against at the end. And you would have lost the chance of providing a strong convincer for the explorer.

5   You would not be able to build the resource state and have nothing to anchor.

6   You would gain a really intense and clear understanding of the nature and dynamics of that Part. If it was one you

wanted to strengthen, then this would be a great process, especially if you identified other supportive Parts to act as mentors.

7   This would be a great way of exploring a relationship through gaining insight into the experience of the other person, plus gaining insight into the nature of the relationship itself. This can be a huge source of information and generate some significant reframes.

8   Some might say the Part is Identity and the Positive Intention is its Spirituality and so is already part of the process. You could take the intention further and ask what this would make possible for you. That could go somewhere interesting. Similarly with the third Part, since it will come with an Identity, and perhaps the elusive mission.

9   You could use the same metaphor throughout, and invite the evolution of this metaphor through time. This would offer a very interesting source of somatic experience as the river flows from stream to ocean, for example, especially if you are working with spatial anchors. Cognitively you could come up with metaphors for each of the elements and develop them in terms of their values and dynamics. This would avoid being personal or going into well worn patterns.

10   This could be great. For each space present a mentor who has something to say. This will give you a space for dissociation. Apart from having a comment about their own particular space, you could invite them into conversation with each other. Since they will be talking about you and what is best for you, you can just listen in and hear what comes up.

11   In Disney Strategy we focus on the Archetypes/Parts. There would be some really interesting information to be had through stepping into the Dream – feeling the strength of its dynamic, energy, direction, and intention. Similarly with the Plan – you would sense it's levels of conviction and doubt. The criticism – you will notice when it is personal and when it is objective. This could be a really useful place to be when you are hearing someone else's dream.

12   One is assuming that 6 Step Reframe is happening in the present. It may be interesting to work with the Part and explore what it did before in the Past, especially if this behaviour is relatively recent. Asking it how it wants to be in the Future gives it real autonomy, without intervention from the Creative Part. It might also reveal the influences of other as yet unseen Parts. Admittedly we may have now invented a new technique!

13   Going second position ONLY once the explorer is resourced allows the explorer put to bed their fear of the Other Person. It enables new information and insight into the possible motives of this person. By not going second, you might be reinforcing the belief that this person is still to be feared, without learning any of the mitigating reasons. Even if the explorer doesn't go fully into second, she will still be close enough to get something new. Discovering that The Other has developed respect for you is a significant moment.

14   If you are wanting to strengthen a belief then working up through the levels would be fantastic: 'in this situation, believing X I am doing … because I am able to … which leads to and means … which enables me to be … so that I can … .

15   For a move away from person, if it is a belief that is not supporting, you could go 'in this situation, believing X, I am unable to do … because I can't … which leads to … and means I am … which stops me from … . Therefore, I want to be able to… which means I am… which results in … because I can … and so now do … in this situation.' Neat!

Linguistic Frames

What are the consequences?

1   The instruction was inviting on-going processing through the use of the continuous tense. You would have freeze framed her insights and not opened the way for more connections.

2   Using first person 'I' invites full association. The explorer doesn't have to convert what she is offered into her own experience, which would happen if you used 'You'. Not disastrous, but you want to avoid anything that weakens full association.

3   Well done. You have understood that the intention was to go for the complex equivalence, and you have gone about it in a different and equally effective way.

4   The first question opens up possibility at skill level and so is future orientated, which provides a future pace. There is also an embedded suggestion with the 'you can'. It is subjective through the use of 'feel'. The second question addresses identity in the present. It requires identifying evidence through the use of 'know'. This could be useful as a calibration question since there will be a finite answer.

5   Much of this depends on how good the trance relationship is, and the intonation of your instruction. Linguistically, the instruction leaves control fully in the hands of the explorer. There might be a slight emphasis on 'step out' and 'move to', but these suggestions would be subtle. Your response removes any linguistic potential of trance.

6   The first instruction takes the person to a future possible Identity, and invites association into this identity with its

Suggested Answers

accompanying reference experience. The second one is merely identifying a wish. It may be part of pattern which goes for the limitations preventing attainment, or even going for submodalities of desire. All very far away from the original intention.

7 The instruction is based in present time, within a narrow frame of 'now'. 'Aware' invites consideration of internal as well as external activity, depending on where the explorer's attention is. It is most likely, however, to be internal. Your question is more externally focussed on behaviours and activities. It potentially invites slight dissociation since the explorer is now talking 'about'.

8 Again good work. The instruction was a pretty precise MO of Possibility challenge. You are seeking to retrieve the same information but in a softer more trance-like manner, especially through the use of the nominalisation 'limitations'. Possibly the instruction should be altered!

9 The instruction using 'that' is placing the sensation in the past, with a presupposition that something happened to it and it has gone. It is inviting the explorer to search for the physiology associated specifically with that sensation and locate it in the past. Your question is very non-specific and has none of this technology, and you could get all sorts of responses which may not address your TOTE.

10 The instruction is deliberately trancy, and has the embedded suggestion 'you now know' and nominalisation 'exploration'. It is also permissive with the presupposition that her exploring will stop. Your instruction misses much of this. While it is still permissive, it doesn't give as clear instructions regarding what 'ready' means.

11 The instruction is looking at process and skills. You've gone for behaviours. Very different information and you would have lost access to information regarding internal strategies.

12 'Onto' and 'at' are very different spatial predicates. 'Onto' takes a higher perspective to the object, whilst 'at' looks across to it. Different information and different submodalities. 'Have realised' places the realisation in the near past so it has already happened. And the explorer is directed to go second position to the Mentor and speak as this person from an associated perspective. It might have been better to preface the instruction with 'As this Mentor ...' just to emphasise this positioning. Your instructions runs the risk that the explorer will respond from her own position, even if you have evoked a Mentor and are assuming that she will move to this perspective. And you have lost the gained awareness.

13 Clearly the response here is required to come from second position and the Mentor's wisdom. The second question invites the response to be received in first position. This might not be a problem if the explorer is in first position at the time and if the hallucination is sufficiently deep so that she can 'hear' what the mentor is saying – but runs the risk of mind reading instead. However, if the explorer is supposedly in second, then this question drags them out of any full association.

14 You can just about get away with your version, assuming the resource is the state in question. Whilst you ask for a description of the connection, you may land lucky and receive information about the process of connecting.

What do you think?

1 By the time you get to Beliefs, you really want your explorer to begin to be accessing her unconscious mind, and not working from the logic of the conscious. This is in preparation for the accessing of the Identity metaphor and then the transportation into the Spirituality space. If you have been auditorily anchoring 'As the Excellent X ...' the process will have begun.

2 When you are arranging the submodalities of the auditorium and viewing room to gain optimum dissociation. Sometimes you may have to resort to metaphor with its sensory predicates – for example a drive-in movie – to establish full dissociation.

3 You have to make sure you clearly enforce second positioning language for each of the positions. You also will be using spatial predicates to mark out location – here and there. And you will need to enforce full association in each position through the use of present tense.

4 Temporal predicates, temporal predicates, temporal predicates until they are coming out of your ears! Plus you will need to follow the sensory predicates of the Timeline's submodality structure or metaphors.

5 The following:

   • Phobia 'Cure' – 'Your unconscious mind wants to protect you from whatever threatens you.' 'If you can take on a phobic reaction so quickly, it stands to reason that you can reverse it just as quick.'

   • Meta Mirror – 'What are you doing so well to continue being like this?'

   • 6 Step Reframe – 'All behaviour has a positive intention.'

6 The following are fantastically elegant ways of unfolding the explorer's deep structure:

   • Meta Model Generalisations – to find out the past and future limitations, the rules and consequences, and the exceptions.

   • Meta Model Distortions – to burst the assumed rules, to challenge the hallucinations of mind read, to test the causal links and reveal the meanings that have been made.

7 This is an easy one – sensory predicates and temporal predicates.

8 Identity requires you to be asking about 'Who are you?' 'You are like what?' 'Your role is …?'   Identity = using the verb To Be.

Do you know your techniques?

	Meta Model	Milton Model	Outcome Frame	Reframing	VAK Predicates	Temporal Predicates	Spatial Predicates Associative/Dissociative
6 Step Reframe			✔	✔			✔
Change Personal History		✔		✔		✔	✔
Circle of Excellence					✔		✔
Disney Strategy		✔					✔
Meta Mirror	✔					✔	✔
Neurological Level Alignment	✔	✔			✔		✔
New Behaviour Generator			✔			✔	✔
Phobia 'Cure'		✔		✔	✔	✔	✔
SCORE	✔	✔				✔	✔
Swish					✔		✔
Timeline Alignment	✔	✔		✔	✔	✔	✔
Visual Squash		✔					✔

Technique Deconstruction

Here you have full deconstructions for the basic techniques to be found within a Practitioner syllabus, plus the two additional ones of **Crossing the Threshold** and **Box 9**.

6 Step Reframe

Purpose: To provide alternatives to an unwanted behaviour.	**Time**: 10-15 mins

Calibrated Evidence: The Part responsible for the behaviour agrees fully congruently to adopt new behaviours.

Model Type	Methodology	Neurological	Linguistic
Natural Complex Model – Parts	Cognitive		Outcome Frame, Associative/ Dissociative Language, Reframing

Skill Emphasis: Establishing and maintaining Rapport with the Part(s) which emerge; Detecting incongruence	**Floor Layout:**

Areas of Concern and Contingencies: Need to pace the Part if it is reluctant to come out. Reassure it that it will not 'get into trouble', which is likely to be its concern since its behaviour is deemed to be unwanted.

The Part may not accept the idea of Positive Intention, so use the As If Frame and say, 'Guess'.

Be prepared for objections. Another Part may feel their role is threatened. If this happens, then you need to introduce a negotiation process.

Be mindful also that not everyone considers they have a Creative Part. So invite 'the Part which comes up with ideas' instead. This saves any installation.

Comments: A very simple process which illustrates the power of Positive Intention and the importance of Rapport.

Change Personal History

Purpose: To remove an undesirable state	**Time**: 10-15 mins

Calibrated Evidence: The Past memory no longer triggers old response. Future pacing triggers new response.

Model Type	Methodology	Neurological	Linguistic
Core Model: Senses – VAK	Cognitive with Kinaesthetic Anchors	Time, Anchoring Association/ Dissociation	Milton Model, Reframing, Spatial and Temporal Predicates Associative/Dissociative Language

Skill Emphasis: Applying discrete Kinaesthetic anchors; Using Trance language intonation	**Floor Layout:**

Areas of Concern and Contingencies: ALWAYS provide an ecology check to start with. If there is any incongruence then use the dissociative form of traveling above the experience, and only going into the event if it is safe to do so.

Need to demonstrate real compassion and admiration for the Younger You who was serving to the very best of his/her ability. Need to be able to reach both Anchor locations easily.

Big danger of the original event being traumatic, or emotionally demanding. You may need to reframe by acknowledging that this response means that it is important and that it will only be temporary. Be prepared to use dissociative language and invite explorer to talk about this Younger You from the present timeframe (without diluting the resource too much). In extreme cases, you may have to provide amnesia through trance.

Comments: quite a demanding process linguistically. Worthwhile going to Bandler's original scripts in Frogs into Princes.

Neurological Level Alignment

Purpose: To strengthen Identity within an identified environment. To generate a powerful resource state and anchor.		**Time**: 45 mins	

Calibrated Evidence: On return to Environment, there is a significant shift in the submodalities from the original inventory.

Model Type	Methodology	Neurological	Linguistic
Complex Model – Neurological Levels	Kinaesthetic	VAK Inventory Mentors Perspectives Metaphor Submodalities Chaining Anchors	Meta Model Milton Model VAK Predicates Spatial Predicates Associative/Dissociative Language

Skill Emphasis:	**Floor Layout:**	
Gathering inventory Maintaining spatial anchors Backtracking Maintaining auditory anchors Using Associative/Dissociative Language Applying Sensory Acuity Using submodalities and assist setting of personal anchor		Spirituality Identity Beliefs and Values Skills Behaviours Environment

Areas of Concern and Contingencies: Make sure with the layout that you leave *half* the space again for the Spirituality space, so that the Explorer can gain a full sensory experience.

Be mindful that Beliefs and Identity are sensitive areas and visiting them can provoke strong emotions.

You have to make sure you clearly separate content between each of the levels. Often Behaviours get confused as Skills. Behaviours are what you can see and hear.

Be prepared for limited fluency at levels that are out of alignment.

Make sure both you and your explorer have the stamina and energy for such a lengthy process.

Comment: This is a complex process and really comes alive the greater the skill levels. Done well, this process becomes the benchmark for all other transformational techniques. It is a real gift to offer someone. Time is included if you consider that the event is some time in the future.

Crossing The Threshold

Purpose: To overcome fear of the Unknown.		**Time**: 20-30 mins	

Calibrated Evidence: The Unknown no longer provokes negative emotion. The threshold point is now much further away.

Model Type	Methodology	Neurological	Linguistic
Constructed Model – Sequential	Kinaesthetic	VAK Perspectives Mentors	Milton Model Spatial Predicates Associative/Dissociative Language

Skill Emphasis: Maintaining the resourcefulness of the Explorer	Floor Layout:
Using spatial anchors and marking by gesture	The Unknown
Using 2nd position language	The Threshold
	The Known

Floor Layout:

The Unknown   Possible Danger

The Threshold ————————————

⬭ ⬭ ⬭ ⬭ Mentors

The Known

Areas of Concern and Contingencies: The explorer will not cross the line until fully resourced. If a mentor is located on the other side of the line, invite the mentor to come over to this side.

Should the explorer falter, ask which mentor needs to offer support. Remind the explorer that he/she can always retrace steps back to the last safe place.

If the fearful place looms too large, you may suggest reducing the submodalities to make it really manageable.

Once the space has been colonised, you can invite your explorer to skip around it as a personal edit, and even step into it.

Comment: A rewarding experience which generates hope and motivation. It provides a reference experience for overcoming fear.

Box 9

Purpose: To rationalise the Unknown and discover the particular area(s) that requires attention.	**Time**: 30 imins

Calibrated Evidence: Only one or two areas are now identified as stressful, and reference experiences can be drawn upon. Some areas prove to be positively beneficial and motivating.

Model Type	Methodology	Neurological	Linguistic
Constructed Model – Sequential	Kinaesthetic	VAK; Submodalities; Metaphor; Perspectives	Milton Model; VAK Predicates; Spatial Predicates; Associative/ Dissociative Language

Skill Emphasis: Keeping the explorer associated in each of the spaces	**Floor Layout:** See the handout layout
Maintaining high levels of sensory acuity and sponsorship since some of the spaces might be uncomfortable	

Areas of Concern and Contingencies: You may want to record your explorer's answers to help them stay on track. It will depend on their level of cognition.

Some of the spaces might be uncomfortable. Ask explorer to stay long enough to find out what exactly the issue is for them and then to step out. You may think that Box 9 will be the most uncomfortable, but that doesn't necessarily follow.

You may need to offer possible examples of situations to activate experience.

Comment: This technique brings up a few surprises, as the explorer discovers that only one or maybe two places in the unknown merit special attention. Makes the crossing over into it much less of an ordeal.

It is offered in a sequential manner. However the explorer can choose, once the territory is marked out, which order of boxes they would rather work through.

Additional Deconstructions

Circle of Excellence

Purpose: To set up and anchor a desired state.			**Time:** 10-15 mins

Calibrated Evidence: Firing the anchor, or even thinking of the anchor, brings back the resourceful state.

Model Type	Methodology	Neurological	Linguistic
Natural Core Model: Senses – VAK Submodalities	Kinaesthetic	Associated/ Dissociated; Anchoring; Submodalities	VAK Predicates; Spatial Predicates; Associative/ Dissociative Language

Skill Emphasis: Using Trance language intonation; Using Associative/Dissociative language	**Floor Layout:**
	Associated Dissociated

Areas of Concern and Contingencies: Explorer may have difficulty hallucinating a circle. They might be able to see a film of themselves, and be able to walk into the picture. Explorer may be intimidated by the word Excellence, and have difficulty locating a reference experience of excellence, through lack of self-belief. Invite examples of momentary excellence, or average brilliance.

Comments: A powerful process in a seemingly unsophisticated structure. Can be incorporated into a more complex technique.

Meta Mirror

Purpose: To find a resourceful response to an unsatisfactory relationship.			**Time**: 30 mins

Calibrated Evidence: At Time $_2$ there is no sign of the physiology of the initial 1st position. Explorer is resourceful and has new insight into the situation, the other person, and their own role in it.

Model Type	Methodology	Neurological	Linguistic
Natural Core Model – Multiple Perspectives/Space	Kinaesthetic	Chaining Anchors Archetypes (if working with Theatre Metaphor) Associated/ Dissociated	Meta Model, Temporal Predicates; Spatial Predicates; Associative/ Dissociative Language

Skill Emphasis: Using associative/dissociative language; Maintaining spatial anchors; Using skills of Sponsorship; Calibrating changes in state and congruence at each position	**Floor Layout :**

Areas of Concern and Contingencies: Only stay in the initial 1st position long enough to calibrate and provide an authentic reference experience. Make sure explorer breaks state.

Only go to 2nd position once full dissociation and a revised 3rd has been achieved. Even then the explorer may not be fully accepting of going full 2nd position, so enable a dissociative 2nd position i.e. looking over shoulder.

You may need to be Fierce to act as a pattern disrupt to the stuck state, speaking up for the Younger Explorer. If full dissociation is not achieved readily, then increase the space either literally or by reducing the submodalities. You may also have to go to 6th or 7th position. Make sure 3rd position swaps places with 1st position, to show Younger Explorer how to do it. Make sure you stack all the anchors by the end.

Comments: Needs to be handled firmly and with precision Managing spatial predicates is essential.

New Behaviour Generator

Purpose: To generate viable alternative behaviours.	**Time:** 20 mins

Calibrated Evidence: There is full congruence when associated into the preferred behaviour. The submodalities will also be at their optimum.

Model Type	Methodology	Neurological	Linguistic
Natural Core Model: Time	Visual	VAK Associated /Dissociated	Outcome Frame; Temporal Predicates; Spatial Predicates; Associative/Dissociative Language

Skill Emphasis: Ensuring accurate eye location; Working with temporal and spatial predicates; Checking signs of incongruence/congruence	**Floor Layout:**

Areas of Concern and Contingencies: You need to make sure that the explorer is actually accessing constructed images from a dissociated position.

Comment: Again a very simple piece of engineering, which can find itself incorporated within larger process.

Phobia 'Cure'

Purpose: To remove a phobic response.	**Time**: 20 mins

Calibrated Evidence: There is no longer a phobic response to the triggers initially fired.

Model Type	Methodology	Neurological	Linguistic
Natural Core Model – Senses Submodalities	Visual	Submodalities; Perspectives	Milton Model, Reframing; VAK Predicates; Temporal and Spatial Predicates; Associative/Dissociative Language

Skill Emphasis: Using Associative/Dissociative Language; Applying Sensory Acuity to detect positive changes in state; Using Submodalities to enhance environment; Using trance intonation, Calibrating altered response	**Floor Layout**: 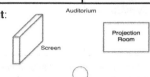

Areas of Concern and Contingencies: Access phobic state for as long as it takes to calibrate.

If there is a difficulty with visualisation, then you may want to act it out spatially.

If the phobia is claustrophobia, make sure the projection room is sufficiently large to be comfortable. If it is vertigo, make sure the projection room is not too high up.

Comment: Often the explorer is left very sceptical of the effectiveness of something quite as simple as this. They may need to go off and discover their different responses in the real world before they accept the change.

Cognitive SCORE: Most suitable for business consultations and coaching as a means of functional problem solving.

Purpose: To clarify the stuck system and identify the appropriate resources to generate change.	**Time**: 30-40mins cognitively

Calibrated Evidence: A realistic Action Plan is drawn up, drawing on identified resources. Any attachment to past causes has disappeared.

Model Type	Methodology	Neurological	Linguistic
Constructed Model – Sequential	Cognitive	Perspectives	Meta Model; Temporal Predicates; Spatial Predicates; Associative/Dissociative Language

Skill Emphasis: Using of Meta Model to gain specific details; Using of temporal predicates to assist full association; Maintaining high level of Rapport	**Floor Layout:** ④ ① ⑤ ② ③ 1 Symptom, 2 Outcome, 3 Effect 4 Cause, 5 Resources

Areas of Concern and Contingencies: Make sure that you follow the sequence as written.

Do not go to Cause until you have a fully associated, resourceful Effect, so that the Outcome/Effect bond is greater than the existing Cause/Symptom bond.

Make sure the explorer is fully associated in the future and past spaces, through using present tense.

Be alert to explorer jumping the gun and mixing locations. Ensure that content specifically relates to the location you are in.

Be mindful that the Cause may be a highly unresourceful place and be prepared to work in close dissociation.

Comment: Pay strict attention to Temporal Predicates to keep Explorer associated.

Dancing the SCORE: More suitable for therapeutic work, where the causes for the behaviour may be distressing

Purpose: To clarify the stuck system and identify the appropriate resources to generate change	**Time**: 20 mins somatically

Calibrated Evidence: The movement is fluid and grounded. The physiology of the Cause is hard to reaccess.

Model Type	Methodology	Neurological	Linguistic
Constructed Model – Sequential	Kinaesthetic -Somatic Syntax	Chaining Anchors	Milton Model; Temporal Predicates; Spatial Predicates; Associative/Dissociative Language

Skill Emphasis: Clear marking out of the space, through use of spatial anchors and temporal predicate Using high level of Rapport Calibrating somatic distinctions	**Floor Layout:** ④ ① ⑤ ② ③ 1 Symptom, 2 Outcome, 3 Effect 4 Cause, 5 Resources

Areas of Concern and Contingencies: Make sure that you follow the sequence as written. **Do not go to Cause** until you have a fully associated, resourceful Effect, so that the Outcome/Effect bond is greater than the existing Cause/Symptom bond. Be mindful that the Cause may be a highly unresourceful place and be prepared to work in close dissociation.

If you are working somatically, pay close attention to micro movement to encourage Explorer to tune into their true position, no matter how self-conscious they may feel initially.

Pay attention to what the explorer's first movements are, since this can provide an enlightening physical metaphor. 'I just had to breathe'.

Pay attention to the space between Symptoms and Outcome as the emergent symbol becomes a powerful resource.

Suggested Answers

Comment: I had some debate about which category of Model to select. Fundamentally it is a time-based model so arguably should be entered as Natural Core Model – Time. But Dilts has taken it beyond Past Present Future. He has identified specific locations within the time continuum. For example *Effects* is not 'Further into the Future': it is a well defined particular subjective point in the future. So for this reason, I have deemed it a Constructed Model – Sequential. Yet because it is in and of itself Time based, time is not a Neurological Frame add on.

I prepared two separate deconstructions for this technique because this is a lovely example of a model being given two different treatments that call upon different skills. This illustrates my fundamental point that it is possible for any Model to spawn a range of techniques, and not just the one the developer presented originally.

The same model can be work through establishing metaphors for each of the states and working through each of these, noticing the changes that take place to the metaphors in the process.

Swish

Purpose: To remove an unwanted behaviour.	**Time**: 30 mins

Calibrated Evidence: Introducing the old trigger no longer fires the undesired thoughts or behaviour.

Model Type	Methodology	Neurological	Linguistic
Natural Core Model: Submodalities	Visual	Associated /Dissociated; Anchoring visually	VAK Predicates; Spatial Predicates; Associative/ Dissociative Language

Skill Emphasis: Encouraging visual representations; Noticing the non-verbal submodalities of each image; Clearly establishing associated and dissociated representations.	**Floor Layout:**

Areas of Concern and Contingencies: If explorer has difficulty visualising, you can work through auditory channels, possibly using a radio tuner as the metaphor.

Comment: Another of the early gems which is based on simple technology, and which can be incorporated into a larger piece.

Timeline Alignment

Purpose: To create a balanced relationship between Past, Present, Future.	**Time**: 30 -45 mins

Calibrated Evidence: There is a balance between Past and Future. Past provides support and 'nudge' to move forwards. Future is a strong attractant.

Model Type	Methodology	Neurological	Linguistic
Natural Core Model: Time	Kinaesthetic	Submodalities; Metaphor; Perspectives; Anchoring	Meta Model; Milton Model; Reframing; VAK Predicates; Temporal Predicates; Spatial Predicates; Associative/Dissociative Language

Skill Emphasis: Using trance language; Maintaining deep rapport with explorer, the structure of the Timeline and the metaphors used; Clearly marking out of the space, with spatial anchors and temporal predicate.	**Floor Layout:** Pre Birth · Past · Present · Future NOTE: Although locations are depicted as circles, apart from the Present, the spaces for the others can be whatever the explorer feels works for him/her.

Areas of Concern and Contingencies: You may find that the explorer has difficulty constructing their Present, which means you need to work to developing the Present before you go any further.

Explorer MUST always be dissociated off the line when going back to Past. Only when Past is fully resourced should any association be attempted.

If at any point there is an abreaction step off the line.

Explorer may experience an emotional point in the revised Future – one of relief, release, disbelief, joy.

Comment: Needs to be managed firmly and with precision. By entering fully into the metaphoric construction you are being offered, you will be able to sustain your predicates and stay in deep rapport.

Only make suggestions re metaphor/submodalities as a means of kick-starting explorer's own thinking.

Visual Squash

Purpose: To resolve inner conflict.			Time: 20 mins

Calibrated Evidence: There is internal calibration and an expression of hope.

Model Type	Methodology	Neurological	Linguistic
Natural Complex Model – Pars	Kinaesthetic	VAK; Collapsing Anchors	Milton Model; Spatial Predicates

Skill Emphasis: Using trance language, Chunkng up to positive intention; Using Parts negotiation if required.	Floor Layout:

Areas of Concern and Contingencies: Give time for the explorer to dvelop awareness of each Part, especially the emergent third one.

Be prepared for some emotional responses arising from the emergence and integration of the third Part into the body.

If you are working with a group, then you may want to extend the integration process by introducing a guided visualisation possibly with background music, or just let the music do the work. I am forever grateful to Lis Mahoney for her gift of Pachebel's Canon in D as the backdrop to some amazing personal revelations when she took me through this process as part of a workshop in Edinburgh.

Comment: This process, which is highly effective and can produce long lasting results, provides an exception to the rule of Sponsorship. Namely it presupposes that the two Parts already in place are not sufficient to do the job. In my map, this is an illustration of when we need to introduce a Part for the requirements of the system as it is today.

Technique Construction

Appraisal of Suggested Techniques

Treatment 1

Why might this work?

1   I am providing a clear set of instructions which appeals to a procedural person.

2   I am asking for reference experiences which is fine for Internally Referenced people.

3   And I am using a cognitive process which is great for the Thinking trait.

4   The exercise can be completed easily in pairs with 10 minutes of each.

What might be the drawbacks of this technique?

1   You could question the selection of these particular coordinates, since they are less well defined. I might need to include definition of terms or else a good preframe to the exercise prior to its presentation.

2   It might have been better to go for Discipline and Freedom. I could possibly provide a selection of both, split the group and see what emerges.

Treatment 2

Why might this work?

1   Again all the traits are being catered for with this process.

2   And, the exercise can be completed easily in pairs with 10 minutes of each.

3   I have covered all of the model, which will provide a deeper description of Ardui's system of excellence.

4   It gives a direct connection between meta model and beliefs, and could throw up some interesting awareness to generate future discussion.

What might be the drawbacks of this technique?

1   Since I have covered more ground, this will require more time for thinking. Involving beliefs is likely to generate the desire for more talking and sharing. This *always* consumes time – unless I offer it content free.

2   The instructions need to be clearly written to avoid confusion.

Treatment 3

Why might this work?

1   Being more thinking than feeling, this could direct their attention more usefully to their less favoured somatic system. It could illustrate the sources of information that come from activating internal representations.

2   It operates from a fully associated perspective, whereas the other two are dissociated, thinking about the process. The former has the possibility of generating a more profound experience and insight, which can then be anchored and act as a reference experience.

3   If they have been used to working this way, then I could invite them to work individually, which would enable the process to be achieved within the time frame.

What might be the drawbacks of this technique?

1   Their inclination to become involved in a kinaesthetic exercise may be determined by when it is scheduled in the day. It would work well if it is following a presentation or previous static cognitive exercises.

2   The instructions need to be clearly written to make sure that the relational field is managed and built up sufficiently.

Writing Instructions

Appraisal of 'Poor' Instructions

Treatment 1

Technical Accuracy
You may need to introduce definitions for Alignment and Performance, to specifically focus attention.
You need to provide the opportunity to identify four different contexts to access the relevant reference experiences.   Pre-frame with 'Think of a time when …'   No need to read out answers since none of them relate to the statement in Step 3. Reading out the answers may in fact cause the explorer to re-anchor a less than resourceful state.

Linguistic Accuracy
Addressing the explorer means the instructions can be read directly and not require changing. Ie use second person and not first person.
At final calibration keeping 'could' still places it in possibility. Changing it to 'can' nails it. You may want to emphasise full association in the future, through the introduction of 'now'.

Constants	Content	Considerations
Title: Yes	Outcome: No	End User: Yes
Source: No	Evidence : No	Layout: Poor
Date: No	Numbered Steps: Yes	Style: OK
Model: Yes	Calibration: No	Meta Comments: No
Length: No	Future Pace: Yes	
Comments	Comments	Comments
Including the model doesn't serve a purpose, especially since it is a cognitive technique.	The exercise is measuring raised self belief in ability to be excellent. Therefore need to use the future event to calibrate the before and after.	No bullet points, no sense of its structure. Space for recording answers needed.

Treatment 2

Technical Accuracy
It covers the rules, limitations, causal links and lost performatives for each of them. The instructions are better written as if they are directly spoken to the explorer. This enables the guide to read them out without having to change the wording at all.

Linguistic Accuracy
Use of comfort as calibration criteria does presuppose that limitations were/are due to discomfort with putting the head above the parapet.
Linguistically the headings are not the same type and therefore the process doesn't flow and loses rhythm. Being, Having are verbs, one of identity and the other, behaviour.   Performance and Discipline are nouns. These differences will activate different responses, and not generate like for like. In some cases the statements are ambiguous – Disciplined people can mean those who have been disciplined, or those who are disciplined.

Constants	Content	Considerations
Title: Yes	Outcome: No	End User: No – written to the Guide
Source: Yes	Evidence: Yes	Layout: Yes see below
Date: Yes	Numbered: Yes	Style: Yes easy to read

Model: referenced and implied	Calibration: Yes	Meta Comments: No
Length: No	Future Pace: Yes	
Comments	Comments	Comments Putting the process into a table helps separate out the steps and keep it visually simple. This also keeps it on A4 page.

Treatment 3

Technical Accuracy
Yes this is technically sound, incorporating somatic syntax, auditory and internal K. It also explores the system inherent in the model, and provides the setup for the creation of a relational field. There are no instructions to set up spatial locations.

Linguistic Accuracy
The Milton waffle at the beginning of the piece is unnecessary. If the explorer is particularly tense, then the guide can draw on his skills and put in softeners as required. Often when this sort of stuff is read out, a trance is certainly induced, but not necessarily a useful one. There is a mix of What's and How's in the steps 1-4. The instructions need to be consistent and therefore all of the same type. Since this is a process model, going for process by using How makes it code congruent. Step 5 uses How consistently.

Constants	Content	Considerations
Title: Yes	Outcome: Yes, hidden within the waffle	End User: Yes
Source: No	Evidence: No	Layout: No differentiation in levels making the process unclear.
Date: No	Numbered: Yes	Style: Waffle in introduction
Model: Yes	Calibration: No starting point	Meta Comments included in the text
Length: Yes	Future Pace: No	
Comments It is essential to acknowledge your sources.	Comments Need to have a calibration to test effectiveness of process, and then the future pace to embed the change and provide neural evidence of change.	Comments Meta Comments should be stripped out and placed as notes. The script should be as stark as possibly without losing effectiveness.

Final Instructions for Treatments and Scenarios

Treatment 1 – Generating Excellence

by Fran Burgess (2011), based on a model devised by Jan Ardui   Time: 20 mins per person

Outcome: To raise levels of excellence

Note: This could be content free, although the explorer might like to have the answers recorded.

Alignment means feeling calm and congruent about your right to be in this situation. Performance relates to the quality of your   behaviours in the task.

1   Think of a task you want to excel at.
- What is your current level of excellence?   1 low-10 high
- How excellent to you think you could be?   1 low-10 high

2   Think of a time when you had poor alignment and poor performance:
- What are you believing?
- What are you valuing?
- What are you like?

3   Think of a time when you had poor alignment and good performance:
- What are you believing?
- What are you valuing?
- What are you like?

4   Think of a time when you had good alignment and poor performance:
- What are you believing?
- What are you valuing?
- What are you like?

5   Think of a time when you had good alignment and good performance:
- What are you believing?
- What are you valuing?
- What are you like?

6   Now consider a task that you want to excel at.   Knowing what you now know, consider the following:
- You are being excellent because you are now believing…
- You are now valuing…
- You are now like …
- How excellent do you think you can be now?   1 low-10 high
- In this situation, what are you now doing differently?

Suggested Answers

Treatment 2 – Generating Excellence

Technique devised by Fran Burgess (2011), based on a model devised by Jan Ardui

Outcome: To raise levels of excellence   Time: 20 mins per person

1   How comfortable are you with the thought of being excellent?   1 low-10 high

2   Complete the following statements.

Being aligned means	Performing well means	Having discipline means	Having freedom means
I can…			
I must…			
Being aligned leads to	**Performing well leads to**	**Having discipline leads to**	**Having freedom leads to**
because…			
since …			
People who are aligned deserve …	**People who perform well deserve …**	**People who are disciplined deserve …**	**People who have freedom deserve …**

3   How comfortable are you now with the thought of being excellent?   1 low-10 high

4   Consider a task or project that is coming up, what challenges are you now prepared to set yourself?

Suggested Answers

Treatment 3 – Generating Excellence

Technique devised by Fran Burgess (2011), based on a model devised by Jan Ardui   Time: 30 mins per person

Outcome: To raise levels of excellence

NOTE: There is no order implied by the sequence of questions. Go with where the explorer wants to go first. Make sure the explorer stays outside of the centre space until invited.

1   Think of a future situation where you want your excellence to be seen.

   • How excellent do you think you can be in this situation?   1 low-10 high

2   Think of a past situation where you were excellent in a way that you felt good about.

   • What is your level of excellence here?   1 low-10 high

3   Working from this experience, step into each of the spaces, in any order, and explore the following

   Discipline:

   • How much discipline are you exercising?   1 low-10 high

   • What does this feel like? Where do you keep this feeling in your body?

   • What gesture sums up your sense of discipline? What phrase comes to mind?

   Freedom:

   • How much freedom are you displaying?   1 low-10 high

   • What does this feel like? Where do you keep this feeling in your body?

   • What gesture sums up your sense of discipline? What phrase comes to mind?

   Performance:

   • How well are you performing ?   1 low-10 high

   • What does this feel like? Where do you keep this feeling in your body?

   • What gesture sums up your sense of discipline? What phrase comes to mind?

   Alignment:

   • How much alignment are you experiencing?

   • What does this feel like? Where do you keep this feeling in your body?

   • What gesture sums up your sense of discipline? What phrase comes to mind?

4   Now step into each of the spaces once more, and the paths between them.

   • What is the relationship between this element and the other three?

   • How are they connected?

   • Has your score altered any?

5   Step into the centre.

   • How high is your level of excellence?   1 low-10 high

   • What does this feel like? Where do you keep this feeling in your body?

   • What gesture sums up your sense of discipline? What phrase comes to mind?

   Anchor this.

6   Enter the future situation. Taking on your Excellence Anchor:

   • What are you seeing, hearing, feeling? What are others seeing, hearing, feeling?

   • What are you doing differently?

   • How excellent are you being in this situation?   1 low-10 high

Suggested Answers

Scenario 1 – Mapping Future Change

Technique devised by Fran Burgess (2011) based on model devised by John Prochaska   Time: 30 mins per person

Outcome: To rehearse and open up the pathways to a desired change.

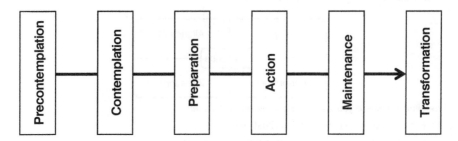

Prochaska's Change Model

1   Consider the change you are contemplating or the change you are in the process of making.
   - How confident are you that you will be fully successful?   1 low-10 high
2   Set the spaces on the floor, and select a time when a change has completely taken place – i.e. giving up smoking.
   - **Precontemplation:** From this perspective become associated in each of the stages.
   - **Associated:** What metaphor describes this situation?
   - **Dissociated:** Looking onto yourself, are you larger, smaller than life or lifesize? In colour or black and white? Directly in front or to either side of you? Moving or still? In focus or fuzzy?
3   Spaces 2 – 6: Repeat the process and keep a record of your answers.
4   Now consider the current desired change.
   - Where you are in the process?
   - Looking on, view the submodalities so far, for each stage in the process – even those stages you haven't reached yet.
   - Transpose the previous submodality patterns onto what you see. Notice how that feels looking at it. Check any elements of incongruence and make adjustments.
5   For the current process, step into each position and take on the metaphor already identified.
   - With this desired change, what is now possible?
6   Walk through the steps and feel the submodality shifts as you go.
   - How does this affect your thinking?
   - How does this affect your state?
7   Once you have a clear representation of the new system, walk through the spaces at least three more times to activate the new neural pathways.
   - What is now possible?
   Returning to present time.
   - How confident are you that you will be fully successful?   1 low-10 high

Scenario 2 – Developing Trust with Another

Model and Technique devised by Fran Burgess (2011)   Time: 20 mins per person

Outcome: To deepen levels of Trust with another.

Note: Check ecology here. There may be issues of abuse. If this is a current working relationship, and there are no reasons to prevent improvement, then it will be safe to engage fully in second position.

1   Identify someone with whom you do not have as sufficiently trusting relationship and you want this to improve.
   • What is your current level of trust with this person?   1 low-10 high
   • What level of respect / commitment / acceptance would you rather have?

2   Set out the following six spaces on the floor.

Me – Ist Position				**The Other – 2nd Position**	
1	Level of Respect Mine for Him/Her		2	Level of Respect His/Her for Me
3	Level of Commitment Mine towards Him/Her		4	Level of Commitment His/hers towards Me
5	Level of Acceptance Mine for Him/Her		6	Level of Acceptance His/Her for Me

3   Following the numbered sequence move from space to space, always returning to the central point. Identify the level you register for each and then ask yourself:
   • How important is this? Does your level need to be raised or lowered?
   • What have been the limiting factors? What can you do differently?
   • How will you know you have reached the optimum level? How will s/he know?
   • What do you want to make sure you continue to have?

4   After each element, return to the centre and ask:
   • What is now possible?
   • What have I learnt?

5   After all six stages, ask yourself:
   • What is your level of trust with this person now?   1 low-10 high
   • How close are you to your optimumlevel of respect / commitment / acceptance for this person?
   • What do you now need to do?

Scenario 3 – Being Equal to Conflict

Technique devised by Fran Burgess (2011)   Time: 10 mins per person

Outcome: To develop the ability to confront conflict

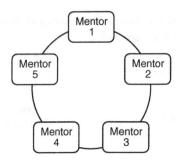

1   Establish a space in the centre. Identify a past, present, or forthcoming situation where you have been or feel unable to confront the person or issue concerned.

   - What is your current level of comfort with conflict?   1 low-10 high

2   Now identify at least 5 mentors who handle conflict in a way that you admire. It might be a work colleague, family member, or it might be someone from history, literature or film – Tom of Tom and Gerry, Gandalf, Martin Luther King, Genghis Khan, Joan of Arc, or any others that come to mind.

3   Once you have established all 5, feel their presence around you.

4   Step into each Mentor, turn and face yourself and, as this person, answer the following questions:

   - What would happen if you didn't confront conflict?

   - What can happen when you do confront conflict?

   - What do you believe about conflict?

   - What resources do you draw on?

5   Each time step back in the centre, receive your mentor's wisdom, making sure you record certainly the last answer.

6   Once all are complete, you can go back and get more information should you need to, or add another mentor or two. Only when you are satisfied, ask yourself:

   - What is your level of comfort with conflict now?   1 low-10 high

   - What can you now do differently?

   - What difference will this make?

7   Identify symbols to represent what what each needs. Set yourself the task of gathering images of each of them, and mount them on paper and post it where you can see it – as your screen saver, by your mirror.

Lightning Source UK Ltd.
Milton Keynes UK
UKOW06f0103161014

240123UK00003B/65/P